# 21 QUALITIES OF
# LEADERS
## IN THE
# BIBLE

DEVELOPING LEADERSHIP TRAITS INSPIRED
*by the* MEN *and* WOMEN *of* SCRIPTURE

# JOHN C.
# MAXWELL

THOMAS NELSON
*Since 1798*

Published in Nashville, Tennessee, by Thomas Nelson. Thomas Nelson is a registered trademark of HarperCollins Christian Publishing, Inc.

Published in association with Yates & Yates, www.yates2.com.

All Scripture quotations are taken from The Holy Bible, New International Version®, NIV®. Copyright © 1973, 1978, 1984, 2011 by Biblica, Inc.® Used by permission. All rights reserved worldwide. www.Zondervan.com. The "NIV" and "New International Version" are trademarks registered in the United States Patent and Trademark Office by Biblica, Inc.®

Thomas Nelson titles may be purchased in bulk for educational, business, fundraising, or sales promotional use. For information, please e-mail SpecialMarkets@ThomasNelson.com.

ISBN 978-0-310-08628-4

First Printing February 2019 / Printed in the United States of America

# CONTENTS

Acknowledgments ................................................................... 7

Introduction ........................................................................... 9

LESSON 1: Character .......................................................... 11

    *David Makes a Choice Based on His Values (1 Samuel 24:1–22)*
    *Daniel's Character Sets Him Apart (Daniel 6:3–26, 28)*
    *Herod's Choices (Matthew 2:1–18)*

LESSON 2: Charisma ........................................................... 23

    *Josiah Celebrates the Passover Like No Other King (2 Chronicles 34:29–33; 35:1–19)*
    *Peter's Charisma (Matthew 16:13–20; Acts 2:14, 22–24, 32–33, 36–41)*
    *Barnabas Grows in Charisma (Acts 4:36–37; 11:20–26; 14:8–18)*

LESSON 3: Commitment ..................................................... 35

    *Ruth—the Great-Grandmother of King David (Ruth 1:3–22)*
    *Caleb and Joshua Will Enter the Promised Land (Numbers 14:1–24; Joshua 14:6–15)*
    *Stephen Pays a Price for Commitment (Acts 6:8–15; 7:1–4, 8–10, 17–25, 29–39, 44–60)*

LESSON 4: Communication ................................................. 49

    *The Decree of Darius (Ezra 6:1–18)*
    *Jesus Models Clear Communication (Matthew 22:23–40)*
    *Paul Argues His Case (Acts 26:1–32)*

LESSON 5: Competence ....................................................... 61

    *Abraham's Obedience with Isaac (Genesis 22:1–18)*
    *Hezekiah Becomes King of Judah (2 Chronicles 29:1–11, 15–36; 31:20–21)*
    *The Qualifications for Overseers and Deacons (1 Timothy 3:1–13)*

LESSON 6: Courage ............................................................. 73

    *Joshua Leads the People Across the Jordan (Joshua 1:1–11; 3:1–4, 14–17)*
    *Elijah on Mount Carmel (1 Kings 18:16–40)*
    *Esther's Courage to Rescue Her People (Esther 3:8–11; 4:1, 4–7, 9–13, 15–16; 5:1–3; 7:3–10)*

LESSON 7: Discernment .......................................................... 85

*Pharaoh Recognizes Joseph's Wisdom (Genesis 41:25–57; 47:13–26)*
*Hiram and Solomon Strike a Deal (1 Kings 5:1–12)*
*Seek Wisdom and You Will Find It (Proverbs 2:1–15)*

LESSON 8: Focus ................................................................... 97

*Nehemiah Ignores the Opposition (Nehemiah 6:1–15)*
*Jesus Helps Peter Regain His Focus (John 21:1–22)*
*Paul Puts His Life in Perspective (Philippians 3:7–14)*

LESSON 9: Generosity .......................................................... 107

*Boaz Gives Willingly (Ruth 2:1–18)*
*The Heart of Giving (Acts 4:32–37; 5:1–11)*
*Paul Encourages Generosity (2 Corinthians 8:1–15)*

LESSON 10: Initiative .......................................................... 117

*Noah's Bold Actions (Genesis 6:9–22; 7:1–5)*
*Isaiah Steps Forward (Isaiah 6:1–13)*
*James Extols the Value of Taking Action (James 2:14–26)*

LESSON 11: Listening .......................................................... 129

*Lessons in Listening (1 Samuel 3:1–21)*
*Inconsistent Listener (2 Chronicles 25:1–2, 5–24, 27–28)*
*Even Jesus Listened and Learned (Luke 2:41–52)*

LESSON 12: Passion ............................................................. 141

*John the Baptist's Fire Is Evident to All (Luke 3:1–18)*
*Whatever You Do . . . (Colossians 3:1–17, 23–24)*
*The Cloud of Witnesses (Hebrews 11:4–12, 22–34; 12:1–3)*

LESSON 13: Positive Attitude ............................................... 153

*A Negative Attitude Dooms a Generation (Numbers 13:1–2, 17–33; 14:1–4, 26–33)*
*Isaiah Paints a Picture of Hope (Isaiah 40:6–15, 21–26, 28–31)*
*Jesus on Asking and Receiving (Matthew 7:7–12)*

LESSON 14: Problem Solving ................................................. 165

*The Shunammite and Elisha (2 Kings 4:8–37)*
*Esther and Mordecai Follow Through (Esther 8:1–14)*
*A Creative Solution (Mark 5:21–34)*

LESSON 15: Relationships ........................................................... 177

    *Jacob Deceives Isaac (Genesis 27:1–45)*
    *The Queen of Sheba Visits Solomon (1 Kings 10:1–10, 13)*
    *Relational Rules from the Apostle Paul (Romans 12:9–21)*

LESSON 16: Responsibility ......................................................... 191

    *David Owns Up (1 Chronicles 21:1–30; 22:1)*
    *Jonah Repents and Gets a Second Chance (Jonah 1:1–17; 2:1–10; 3:1–10)*
    *Pilate Washes His Hands (Matthew 27:11–26)*

LESSON 17: Security ................................................................... 205

    *Moses and His Siblings (Numbers 12:1–15)*
    *Saul Fears David's Success (1 Samuel 18:1–16)*
    *Nathan Rebukes a King (2 Samuel 12:1–19)*

LESSON 18: Self-Discipline ........................................................ 217

    *The Psalmist Prays for Self-Discipline (Psalm 119:1–16)*
    *Jesus Prepares to Start His Ministry (Luke 4:1–21)*
    *Paul's Advice (1 Corinthians 9:24–27; 10:1–13, 23–24)*

LESSON 19: Servanthood ........................................................... 229

    *David Stands Up for the Men Who Stayed Behind (1 Samuel 30:1–31)*
    *The Samaritan Stops to Help (Luke 10:25–37)*
    *Jesus Provides the Ultimate Visual Aid (John 13:1–17)*

LESSON 20: Teachability ............................................................ 241

    *King Nebuchadnezzar Learns the Hard Way (Daniel 4:4–37)*
    *Naaman Chose Wisely (2 Kings 5:1–15)*
    *The Next Lesson (Mark 10:17–27)*

LESSON 21: Vision ..................................................................... 253

    *The Vision of Abram (Genesis 12:1–7; 15:1–21)*
    *The Vision Given to Moses Lasted for Millennia (Exodus 12:1–29)*
    *A Vision for All Time (Matthew 28:16–20)*

Final Group Discussion Questions ........................................... 265
About the Author ....................................................................... 266

# ACKNOWLEDGMENTS

I want to say thank you to Charlie Wetzel and the rest of the team who assisted me with the formation and publication of this book. And to the people in my organizations who support it. You all add incredible value to me, which allows me to add value to others. Together, we're making a difference!

# INTRODUCTION

Early in my career when I first began teaching people in church about leadership, they were often surprised. I was clearly young and inexperienced, yet the ideas I was able to convey seemed to be beyond what I should know. By my late twenties, I sensed God wanted me to teach about leadership for the rest of my life. It was my calling and my passion.

As I started writing and speaking on leadership to a more general audience, people would ask, "Where in the world did you learn all this?" I was happy to let them in on a secret: everything I know about leadership I learned from the Bible.

Not only is the Bible the greatest book ever written, it is the greatest *leadership* book ever written. Everything you could ever want to learn about leadership—vision, purpose, thinking strategy, communication, attitude, encouragement, mentoring, follow-through—is all there. You just need to be open to what God wants to teach you. As it says in Isaiah 55:11,

> *My word that goes out from my mouth:*
>    *It will not return to me empty,*
> *but will accomplish what I desire*
>    *and achieve the purpose for which I sent it.*

God's word always fulfills his purpose. If you have felt a stirring to become a better leader or if someone has tapped your shoulder and asked you to lead, God will help you.

I am excited for you as you begin this journey of leadership development through the Word of God. The focus of this workbook is on the qualities that every person needs to develop to become a better leader. I've based this study on my book *The 21 Indispensable Qualities of a Leader: Becoming the Person Others Will Want to Follow.* Each lesson begins with a definition of the quality, but the main focus is on how that quality impacts the leadership of people in the Bible. Each lesson contains three carefully selected biblical case studies—some positive, some negative—that reveal and illustrate the quality. After you read each of these passages from the Bible, you will answer study questions that will prompt you to really dig into the Scripture and learn about leadership from it.

But this workbook isn't meant to be a theoretical study. It's meant to help you *become* a better leader—the kind of person others want to follow. So every section contains leadership insight and reflection questions as well as a prompt for taking action so that you can develop the leadership quality in your life.

You can easily go through this workbook on your own and improve your leadership ability. But I want to encourage you to do this with a group. There's nothing like learning with other like-minded people who desire to grow and develop their leadership skills. To help you with this process, I've included group discussion questions at the end of each lesson. Plus, I've included one additional set of questions the group can answer after you've completed all twenty-one lessons.

My recommendation is that you gather a group of people to engage in the process together. Before you meet, everyone should complete the lesson. Then gather together as a group and answer the discussion questions. I believe you'll find you learn better and enjoy it more when you can discuss what you've learned and hold one another accountable to grow.

May God bless you as you enjoy this journey.

# CHARACTER

## Be a Piece of the Rock

## THE QUALITY DEFINED

Leaders cannot rise above the limitations of their character. That's because followers do not trust leaders whose character they know to be flawed, and they will not continue following those leaders.

Your character determines who you are. Who you are determines what you see. What you see determines what you do. That's why you can never separate a leader's character from his actions. If a leader's actions and intentions are continually working against each other, then you can examine the individual's character to find out why.

How a leader deals with the circumstances of life tells you a lot about his character. Crisis doesn't necessarily make character, but it certainly does reveal it. Adversity is a crossroads which makes a person choose one of two paths: character or compromise. Every time he chooses character, he becomes stronger, even if that choice brings negative consequences. The development of character is at the heart of our development, not just as leaders, but as human beings.

There are a lot of things in life that we have no control over. But we do choose our character. In fact, we create it every time we make choices—to cop out or dig out of a hard situation, to bend the truth or stand under the weight of it, to take the easy money or pay the price. As you live your life and make choices today, you are continuing to create your character.

# CASE STUDIES

Read these case studies from the Bible and answer the study questions that follow.

## ❶ David Makes a Choice Based on His Values

### 1 Samuel 24:1–22

*1 After Saul returned from pursuing the Philistines, he was told, "David is in the Desert of En Gedi." 2 So Saul took three thousand able young men from all Israel and set out to look for David and his men near the Crags of the Wild Goats.*

*3 He came to the sheep pens along the way; a cave was there, and Saul went in to relieve himself. David and his men were far back in the cave. 4 The men said, "This is the day the LORD spoke of when he said to you, 'I will give your enemy into your hands for you to deal with as you wish.'" Then David crept up unnoticed and cut off a corner of Saul's robe.*

*5 Afterward, David was conscience-stricken for having cut off a corner of his robe. 6 He said to his men, "The LORD forbid that I should do such a thing to my master, the LORD's anointed, or lay my hand on him; for he is the anointed of the LORD." 7 With these words David sharply rebuked his men and did not allow them to attack Saul. And Saul left the cave and went his way.*

*8 Then David went out of the cave and called out to Saul, "My lord the king!" When Saul looked behind him, David bowed down and prostrated himself with his face to the ground. 9 He said to Saul, "Why do you listen when men say, 'David is bent on harming you'? 10 This day you have seen with your own eyes how the LORD delivered you into my hands in the cave. Some urged me to kill you, but I spared you; I said, 'I will not lay my hand on my lord, because he is the LORD's anointed.' 11 See, my father, look at this piece of your robe in my hand! I cut off the corner of your robe but did not kill you. See that there is nothing in my hand to indicate that I am guilty of wrongdoing or rebellion. I have not wronged you, but you are hunting me down to take my life. 12 May the LORD judge between you and me. And may the Lord avenge the wrongs you have done to me, but my hand will not touch you. ¹³ As the old saying goes, 'From evildoers come evil deeds,' so my hand will not touch you.*

*¹⁴ "Against whom has the king of Israel come out? Who are you pursuing? A dead dog? A flea? ¹⁵ May the LORD be our judge and decide between us. May he consider my cause and uphold it; may he vindicate me by delivering me from your hand."*

*¹⁶ When David finished saying this, Saul asked, "Is that your voice, David my son?" And he wept aloud. ¹⁷ "You are more righteous than I," he said. "You have treated me well, but I have treated you badly. ¹⁸ You have just now told me about the good you did to me; the LORD delivered me into your hands, but you did not kill me. ¹⁹ When a man finds his enemy, does he let him get away unharmed? May the LORD reward you well for the way you treated me today. ²⁰ I know that you will surely be king and that the kingdom of Israel will be established in your hands. ²¹ Now swear to me by the LORD that you will not kill off my descendants or wipe out my name from my father's family."*

*²² So David gave his oath to Saul. Then Saul returned home, but David and his men went up to the stronghold.*

## Study Questions

1. David refused to kill King Saul because he was the Lord's anointed. However, David had also been anointed by the prophet Samuel as Israel's future king (see 1 Samuel 16:13). Do you think David would have been within his rights to kill Saul and take his place? Explain.

_____

_____

_____

_____

_____

_____

2. If David had killed Saul, how might that have impacted David's future as a king? How does the way a leader gains his position impact the tone of his leadership?

_____

_____

_____

3. David's men wanted him to kill Saul. Do you think David's decision not to strike down Saul frustrated his men or made them admire him? Explain.

_____

_____

_____

4. Why do you think Saul asked David to swear not to kill his descendants rather than swearing not to kill him? What does his request tell you about the two men?

_____

_____

_____

# ② Daniel's Character Sets Him Apart

## Daniel 6:3–26, 28

*³ Now Daniel so distinguished himself among the administrators and the satraps by his exceptional qualities that the king planned to set him over the whole kingdom. ⁴ At this, the administrators and the satraps tried to find grounds for charges against Daniel in his conduct of government* affairs, but they were unable to do so. They could find no corruption in him, because he was trustworthy and neither corrupt nor negligent. *5 Finally these men said, "We will never find any basis for charges against this man Daniel unless it has something to do with the law of his God."*

*6 So these administrators and satraps went as a group to the king and said:* "May King Darius live forever! *7 The royal administrators, prefects, satraps, advisers and governors have all agreed that the king should issue an edict and enforce the decree that anyone who prays to any god or human being during the next thirty days, except to you, Your Majesty, shall be thrown into the lions' den. *8 Now, Your Majesty, issue the decree and put it in writing so that it cannot be altered—in accordance with the law of the Medes and Persians, which cannot be repealed."* *9 So King Darius put the decree in writing.*

*10 Now when Daniel learned that the decree had been published, he went home to his upstairs room where the windows opened toward Jerusalem. Three times a day he got down on his knees and prayed, giving thanks to his God, just as he had done before. *11 Then these men went as a group and found Daniel praying and asking God for help. *12 So they went to the king and spoke to him about his royal decree:* "Did you not publish a decree that during the next thirty days anyone who prays to any god or human being except to you, Your Majesty, would be thrown into the lions' den?"*

The king answered, "The decree stands—in accordance with the law of the Medes and Persians, which cannot be repealed."*

*13 Then they said to the king,* "Daniel, who is one of the exiles from Judah, pays no attention to you, Your Majesty, or to the decree you put in writing. He still prays three times a day."* *14 When the king heard this, he was greatly distressed; he was determined to rescue Daniel and made every effort until sundown to save him.*

*15 Then the men went as a group to King Darius and said to him,* "Remember, Your Majesty, that according to the law of the Medes and Persians no decree or edict that the king issues can be changed."*

*16 So the king gave the order, and they brought Daniel and threw him into the lions' den. The king said to Daniel,* "May your God, whom you serve continually, rescue you!"*

*17 A stone was brought and placed over the mouth of the den, and the king sealed it with his own signet ring and with the rings of his nobles, so that Daniel's situation might not be changed. 18 Then the king returned to his palace and spent the night without eating and without any entertainment being brought to him. And he could not sleep.*

*19 At the first light of dawn, the king got up and hurried to the lions' den. 20 When he came near the den, he called to Daniel in an anguished voice, "Daniel, servant of the living God, has your God, whom you serve continually, been able to rescue you from the lions?"*

*21 Daniel answered, "May the king live forever! 22 My God sent his angel, and he shut the mouths of the lions. They have not hurt me, because I was found innocent in his sight. Nor have I ever done any wrong before you, Your Majesty."*

*23 The king was overjoyed and gave orders to lift Daniel out of the den. And when Daniel was lifted from the den, no wound was found on him, because he had trusted in his God.*

*24 At the king's command, the men who had falsely accused Daniel were brought in and thrown into the lions' den, along with their wives and children. And before they reached the floor of the den, the lions overpowered them and crushed all their bones.*

*25 Then King Darius wrote to all the nations and peoples of every language in all the earth:*

*"May you prosper greatly!*

*26 "I issue a decree that in every part of my kingdom people must fear and reverence the God of Daniel.". . .*

*28 So Daniel prospered during the reign of Darius and the reign of Cyrus the Persian.*

## Study Questions

1. Why do you think the other officials decided to take action against Daniel? What was their motivation?

_____

_____

_____

_____

2. Daniel is described as being neither corrupt nor negligent. How well does the absence of these two traits describe good character? What additional traits would you add to that list?

_____

_____

_____

_____

_____

_____

3. Why do you think Daniel continued to pray to God three times a day after Darius signed the edict?

_____

_____

_____

_____

_____

_____

4. How do you think Darius would have responded if he had found Daniel dead the next morning? What, if anything, would have changed? List the things God achieved by saving Daniel.

_____

_____

_____

_____

_____

_____

## ❸ Herod's Choices

### Matthew 2:1–18

*¹After Jesus was born in Bethlehem in Judea, during the time of King Herod, Magi from the east came to Jerusalem ² and asked, "Where is the one who has been born king of the Jews? We saw his star when it rose and have come to worship him."*

*³ When King Herod heard this he was disturbed, and all Jerusalem with him. ⁴ When he had called together all the people's chief priests and teachers of the law, he asked them where the Messiah was to be born. ⁵ "In Bethlehem in Judea," they replied, "for this is what the prophet has written:*

> *⁶ "'But you, Bethlehem, in the land of Judah,*
>> *are by no means least among the rulers of Judah;*
> *for out of you will come a ruler*
>> *who will shepherd my people Israel.'"*

*⁷ Then Herod called the Magi secretly and found out from them the exact time the star had appeared. ⁸ He sent them to Bethlehem and said, "Go and search carefully for the child. As soon as you find him, report to me, so that I too may go and worship him."*

*⁹ After they had heard the king, they went on their way, and the star they had seen when it rose went ahead of them until it stopped over the place where the child was. ¹⁰ When they saw the star, they were overjoyed. ¹¹ On coming to the house, they saw the child with his mother Mary, and they bowed down and worshiped him. Then they opened their treasures and presented him with gifts of gold, frankincense and myrrh. ¹² And having been warned in a dream not to go back to Herod, they returned to their country by another route.*

*¹³ When they had gone, an angel of the Lord appeared to Joseph in a dream. "Get up," he said, "take the child and his mother and escape to Egypt. Stay there until I tell you, for Herod is going to search for the child to kill him."*

*¹⁴ So he got up, took the child and his mother during the night and left for Egypt, ¹⁵ where he stayed until the death of Herod. And so was fulfilled what the Lord had said through the prophet: "Out of Egypt I called my son."*

*¹⁶ When Herod realized that he had been outwitted by the Magi, he was furious, and he gave orders to kill all the boys in Bethlehem and its vicinity who were two years old and under, in accordance with the time he had learned from the Magi.*

*¹⁷ Then what was said through the prophet Jeremiah was fulfilled:*

*¹⁸ "A voice is heard in Ramah,*
*weeping and great mourning,*
*Rachel weeping for her children*
*and refusing to be comforted,*
*because they are no more."*

## Study Questions

1. The passage says King Herod and all Jerusalem were disturbed by the magi's question regarding the birth of a king of the Jews. Why was Herod so disturbed? Why were the people of Jerusalem?

_____

_____

_____

2. What do you think Herod would have done if the magi had returned to him and given him the information he requested?

_____

_____

_____

_____

3. What actions of Herod are indications of his character? List them. Beside each action, describe what aspect of his character it reveals.

_____

_____

_____

_____

_____

# Leadership Insight and Reflection

What were the motives of the various leaders in these passages?

David: _____

Saul: _____

Daniel: _____

Darius: _____

The Administrators and Satraps: _____

Herod: _____

The Magi: _____

How are motives and character connected? How do they interact with one another? Can a leader have bad motives but good character? Or good motives but bad character? Think about each of the following leadership combinations and describe what that type would do.

Bad Motives—Good Character

_____

_____

_____

Bad Motives—Bad Character

_____

_____

_____

Good Motives—Bad Character

_____

_____

_____

Good Motives—Good Character

_____

_____

_____

# TAKING ACTION

Take some time to analyze your motivation for leading others. What would you say you are trying to accomplish as a leader?

_____

_____

_____

_____

_____


Go back to the description of character in Daniel with any additional traits you named. Assess yourself in these areas:

Not Corrupt:_____

Not Negligent: _____

_____ : _____

_____ : _____

_____ : _____

_____ : _____

Where do you need to grow so that your character and motives are positive and strong?

_____

_____

_____


What will you do to change?

_____

_____

_____

_____

# GROUP DISCUSSION QUESTIONS

1. David is described as a man after God's own heart (see 1 Samuel 13:14). How much of that description do you think relates to David's character?

2. If you had been in David's situation, what would you have done?

   ❑ Strike down Saul yourself
   ❑ Allow your men to strike down Saul
   ❑ Confront Saul in the cave
   ❑ Cut Saul's robe and address Saul afterward (as David did)
   ❑ Cut Saul's robe but not speak to him
   ❑ Stay hidden entirely and wait for Saul to leave

   Explain your answer.

3. In Daniel 6:14, we read that King Darius "was determined to rescue Daniel and made every effort until sundown to save him." What do you think that might have involved? Why didn't he just suspend the edict?

4. What do you think Daniel's mindset was when he was put into the lion's den? Do you think he expected to be saved or to die? Explain.

5. In two of the passages, God sent angels to intervene for his people. When you find yourself in a difficult situation, how does your character come into play? And what do you expect God to do on your behalf?

6. What was your greatest takeaway about character in leadership from this lesson?

7. What action do you believe God is asking you to take in your leadership as a result? When and how will you do it?

LESSON 2

# CHARISMA

## The First Impression Can Seal the Deal

### THE QUALITY DEFINED

Most people think of charisma as something mystical, almost undefinable. They think it's a quality that comes at birth or not at all. But that's not entirely true. Charisma, plainly stated, is the ability to draw people to you. And like other character traits, it can be developed.

Think of the people you want to spend time with. How would you describe them? Moody? Insecure? Cynical? Of course not. Charismatic people are celebrators. They're passionate about life. They expect and assume the best of others. They give of themselves. They share wisdom, resources, and even their special occasions. If you want to attract others, you need to be like the people you enjoy being with. Appreciate others, encourage them, and help them reach their potential, and they will love you for it.

A charismatic person's positive traits are apparent the first time you meet them, making them immediately attractive. But charismatic *leadership* continues beyond the first impression. To positively influence people in the long term, a charismatic leader is consistent. He or she makes people feel liked, valued, and appreciated on a day-to-day basis.

When it comes to charisma, the bottom line is other-mindedness. Leaders who continually think about others and their concerns before thinking of themselves will be attractive to people. And they will build loyalty in their followers.

# CASE STUDIES

Read these case studies from the Bible and answer the study questions that follow.

## ① Josiah Celebrates the Passover Like No Other King

### 2 Chronicles 34:29–33

*29 Then the king called together all the elders of Judah and Jerusalem.
30 He went up to the temple of the LORD with the people of Judah, the
inhabitants of Jerusalem, the priests and the Levites—all the people from
the least to the greatest. He read in their hearing all the words of the
Book of the Covenant, which had been found in the temple of the LORD.
31 The king stood by his pillar and renewed the covenant in the presence of
the LORD—to follow the LORD and keep his commands, statutes and decrees
with all his heart and all his soul, and to obey the words of the covenant
written in this book.*

*32 Then he had everyone in Jerusalem and Benjamin pledge themselves
to it; the people of Jerusalem did this in accordance with the covenant of God,
the God of their ancestors.*

*33 Josiah removed all the detestable idols from all the territory belonging
to the Israelites, and he had all who were present in Israel serve the LORD
their God. As long as he lived, they did not fail to follow the LORD, the God of
their ancestors.*

### 2 Chronicles 35:1–19

*1 Josiah celebrated the Passover to the LORD in Jerusalem, and the Passover
lamb was slaughtered on the fourteenth day of the first month. 2 He appointed
the priests to their duties and encouraged them in the service of the LORD's
temple. 3 He said to the Levites, who instructed all Israel and who had been
consecrated to the LORD: "Put the sacred ark in the temple that Solomon son
of David king of Israel built. It is not to be carried about on your shoulders.
Now serve the LORD your God and his people Israel. 4 Prepare yourselves by*

families in your divisions, according to the instructions written by David king of Israel and by his son Solomon.

⁵ "Stand in the holy place with a group of Levites for each subdivision of the families of your fellow Israelites, the lay people. ⁶ Slaughter the Passover lambs, consecrate yourselves and prepare the lambs for your fellow Israelites, doing what the LORD commanded through Moses."

⁷ Josiah provided for all the lay people who were there a total of thirty thousand lambs and goats for the Passover offerings, and also three thousand cattle—all from the king's own possessions.

⁸ His officials also contributed voluntarily to the people and the priests and Levites. Hilkiah, Zechariah and Jehiel, the officials in charge of God's temple, gave the priests twenty-six hundred Passover offerings and three hundred cattle. ⁹ Also Konaniah along with Shemaiah and Nethanel, his brothers, and Hashabiah, Jeiel and Jozabad, the leaders of the Levites, provided five thousand Passover offerings and five hundred head of cattle for the Levites.

¹⁰ The service was arranged and the priests stood in their places with the Levites in their divisions as the king had ordered. ¹¹ The Passover lambs were slaughtered, and the priests splashed against the altar the blood handed to them, while the Levites skinned the animals. ¹² They set aside the burnt offerings to give them to the subdivisions of the families of the people to offer to the LORD, as it is written in the Book of Moses. They did the same with the cattle. ¹³ They roasted the Passover animals over the fire as prescribed, and boiled the holy offerings in pots, caldrons and pans and served them quickly to all the people. ¹⁴ After this, they made preparations for themselves and for the priests, because the priests, the descendants of Aaron, were sacrificing the burnt offerings and the fat portions until nightfall. So the Levites made preparations for themselves and for the Aaronic priests.

¹⁵ The musicians, the descendants of Asaph, were in the places prescribed by David, Asaph, Heman and Jeduthun the king's seer. The gatekeepers at each gate did not need to leave their posts, because their fellow Levites made the preparations for them.

¹⁶ So at that time the entire service of the LORD was carried out for the celebration of the Passover and the offering of burnt offerings on the altar of the LORD, as King Josiah had ordered. ¹⁷ The Israelites who were present

*celebrated the Passover at that time and observed the Festival of Unleavened Bread for seven days. <sup>18</sup> The Passover had not been observed like this in Israel since the days of the prophet Samuel; and none of the kings of Israel had ever celebrated such a Passover as did Josiah, with the priests, the Levites and all Judah and Israel who were there with the people of Jerusalem. <sup>19</sup> This Passover was celebrated in the eighteenth year of Josiah's reign.*

## Study Questions

1. Josiah ordered that the temple be repaired, and while that was being done, the Book of the Law was discovered. Josiah repented when he learned its contents. His reverence for God motivated him to observe the Passover. But he was also concerned about the people. What evidence can you find in the passage that Josiah was other-minded?

_____

_____

_____

_____

2. How does the response of Josiah's officials imply that Josiah possessed charisma?

_____

_____

_____

_____

_____

3. What made this event memorable to the people of Israel? How do you think you would have felt had you been present? What would have been your opinion of Josiah?

_____

_____

_____

_____

_____

# ② Peter's Charisma

## Matthew 16:13–20

*13 When Jesus came to the region of Caesarea Philippi, he asked his disciples, "Who do people say the Son of Man is?"*

*14 They replied, "Some say John the Baptist; others say Elijah; and still others, Jeremiah or one of the prophets."*

*15 "But what about you?" he asked. "Who do you say I am?"*

*16 Simon Peter answered, "You are the Messiah, the Son of the living God."*

*17 Jesus replied, "Blessed are you, Simon son of Jonah, for this was not revealed to you by flesh and blood, but by my Father in heaven. 18 And I tell you that you are Peter, and on this rock I will build my church, and the gates of Hades will not overcome it. 19 I will give you the keys of the kingdom of heaven; whatever you bind on earth will be bound in heaven, and whatever you loose on earth will be loosed in heaven." 20 Then he ordered his disciples not to tell anyone that he was the Messiah.*

## Acts 2:14, 22–24, 32–33, 36–41

*14 Then Peter stood up with the Eleven, raised his voice and addressed the crowd: "Fellow Jews and all of you who live in Jerusalem, let me explain this to you; listen carefully to what I say. . . .*

*22 "Fellow Israelites, listen to this: Jesus of Nazareth was a man accredited by God to you by miracles, wonders and signs, which God did among you through him, as you yourselves know. 23 This man was handed over to you by God's deliberate plan and foreknowledge; and you, with the help of wicked men, put him to death by nailing him to the cross. 24 But God raised him from the dead, freeing him from the agony of death, because it was impossible for death to keep its hold on him. . . .*

*32 God has raised this Jesus to life, and we are all witnesses of it. 33 Exalted to the right hand of God, he has received from the Father the promised Holy Spirit and has poured out what you now see and hear. . . .*

*36 "Therefore let all Israel be assured of this: God has made this Jesus, whom you crucified, both Lord and Messiah."*

37 When the people heard this, they were cut to the heart and said to Peter and the other apostles, "Brothers, what shall we do?"

38 Peter replied, "Repent and be baptized, every one of you, in the name of Jesus Christ for the forgiveness of your sins. And you will receive the gift of the Holy Spirit. 39 The promise is for you and your children and for all who are far off—for all whom the Lord our God will call."

40 With many other words he warned them; and he pleaded with them, "Save yourselves from this corrupt generation." 41 Those who accepted his message were baptized, and about three thousand were added to their number that day.

## Study Questions

1. What do you think Peter's motivation was when Jesus asked the disciples who they thought he was and Peter declared that Jesus was the messiah? What was Peter's motivation when he later addressed the Israelites and declared that Jesus was the messiah? What does his change in motivation show?

_____

_____

_____

_____

_____

_____

2. How is the crowd's response to Peter an indication of his charisma?

_____

_____

_____

_____

_____

_____

_____

3. Peter had the advantage of knowing and communicating truth when he spoke and wanting to help the people. How are leaders who don't tell the truth or care about people able to use charisma to their advantage?

_____

_____

_____

_____

_____

_____

4. Do you think Peter was always charismatic as a leader? Did he develop greater charisma over time? What do you think?

_____

_____

_____

_____

# ❸ Barnabas Grows in Charisma

## Acts 4:36–37

³⁶ *Joseph, a Levite from Cyprus, whom the apostles called Barnabas (which means "son of encouragement"), ³⁷ sold a field he owned and brought the money and put it at the apostles' feet.*

## Acts 11:20–26

²⁰ *Some of them, however, men from Cyprus and Cyrene, went to Antioch and began to speak to Greeks also, telling them the good news about the*

*Lord Jesus.* <sup>21</sup> *The Lord's hand was with them, and a great number of people believed and turned to the Lord.*

<sup>22</sup> *News of this reached the church in Jerusalem, and they sent Barnabas to Antioch.* <sup>23</sup> *When he arrived and saw what the grace of God had done, he was glad and encouraged them all to remain true to the Lord with all their hearts.* <sup>24</sup> *He was a good man, full of the Holy Spirit and faith, and a great number of people were brought to the Lord.*

<sup>25</sup> *Then Barnabas went to Tarsus to look for Saul,* <sup>26</sup> *and when he found him, he brought him to Antioch. So for a whole year Barnabas and Saul met with the church and taught great numbers of people. The disciples were called Christians first at Antioch.*

## Acts 14:8–18

<sup>8</sup> *In Lystra there sat a man who was lame. He had been that way from birth and had never walked.* <sup>9</sup> *He listened to Paul as he was speaking. Paul looked directly at him, saw that he had faith to be healed* <sup>10</sup> *and called out, "Stand up on your feet!" At that, the man jumped up and began to walk.*

<sup>11</sup> *When the crowd saw what Paul had done, they shouted in the Lycaonian language, "The gods have come down to us in human form!"* <sup>12</sup> *Barnabas they called Zeus, and Paul they called Hermes because he was the chief speaker.* <sup>13</sup> *The priest of Zeus, whose temple was just outside the city, brought bulls and wreaths to the city gates because he and the crowd wanted to offer sacrifices to them.*

<sup>14</sup> *But when the apostles Barnabas and Paul heard of this, they tore their clothes and rushed out into the crowd, shouting:* <sup>15</sup> *"Friends, why are you doing this? We too are only human, like you. We are bringing you good news, telling you to turn from these worthless things to the living God, who made the heavens and the earth and the sea and everything in them.* <sup>16</sup> *In the past, he let all nations go their own way.* <sup>17</sup> *Yet he has not left himself without testimony: He has shown kindness by giving you rain from heaven and crops in their seasons; he provides you with plenty of food and fills your hearts with joy."* <sup>18</sup> *Even with these words, they had difficulty keeping the crowd from sacrificing to them.*

## Study Questions

1. What does it say about Barnabas' charisma that the people of Lystra thought he was Zeus, the king of the gods in Greek culture, even though Barnabas had not performed any miracles?

_____

_____

_____

_____

_____

_____

_____

2. Barnabas' original name was Joseph. What does it say about him that the apostles called him "son of encouragement"? What do you think his role was with the twelve in Jerusalem?

_____

_____

_____

_____

_____

_____

3. Why was Barnabas such a good encourager? What traits do you see that made him able to do what he did and attract people to himself?

_____

_____

_____

_____

_____

_____

_____

# LEADERSHIP INSIGHT AND REFLECTION

All three of the leaders in these passages had the truth on their side. It was at the foundation of what they were trying to accomplish. How does that give someone a leg up when it comes to leading others?

_____

_____

_____

_____

_____

_____

_____

_____

All three of these leaders desired to help others. How does a leader's motivation come into play when it comes to developing charisma?

_____

_____

_____

_____

_____

_____

_____

What is your foundation for leading? And what is your motivation? What are you trying to accomplish with your leadership?

_____

_____

_____

_____

_____

_____

_____

# TAKING ACTION

Think about your answers to the last two questions. Is there any inconsistency between God's truth and your leadership methods? Are your motives pure? Do you lead out of a desire to help others? Are you focused on people or your own agenda? What are you sensing that God wants you to change to become a better leader? What can you do immediately to improve?

_____

_____

_____

_____

_____

_____

_____

_____

_____

_____

_____

_____

_____

_____

_____

_____

_____

_____

_____

_____

_____

_____

# Group Discussion Questions

1. Were you able to relate to the sacrificial system of the Old Testament temple—could you relate to Josiah's desire to sacrifice so many animals and his officials' desire to give additional animals to be sacrificed? What would be a modern-day equivalent?

2. Josiah, Peter, and Barnabas all had different levels of formal authority. What does this say about the role of formal authority when it comes to charisma? How would you define each leader's position, title, or authority and how much significance it had?

3. In the past, have you considered charisma a natural gift or a developable trait? Explain.

4. How much natural charisma do you think each of the three leaders had? How much was developed?

5. How much natural charisma do you consider yourself to have? How would you rate yourself on a scale from one (low) to ten (high)?

6. What have you done to make yourself more likeable and charismatic? Have you been able to increase your likeability while maintaining high standards? Explain.

7. What action do you believe you could take to improve your charisma? When and how will you do it?

# LESSON 3

# COMMITMENT

## It Separates Doers from Dreamers

## THE QUALITY DEFINED

The world has never seen a great leader who lacked commitment. That's because true commitment inspires and attracts others. Followers need to know they can count on their leader, and commitment communicates that.

Great commitment always precedes great achievement. But many people want everything to be perfect before they're willing to commit themselves to anything. This will automatically defeat them, because a half-hearted attempt rarely succeeds. The necessary steps are commitment, then action, then achievement.

When it comes to commitment, there are really only four types of people:

1. **Cop Outs:** people who have no goals and do not commit;
2. **Hold Outs:** people who don't know if they can reach their goals, so they're afraid to commit;
3. **Drop Outs:** people who start toward a goal but quit when the going gets tough; and
4. **All Outs:** People who set goals, commit to them, and pay the price to reach them.

To increase your level of commitment, it's important first to measure where it is right now. Sometimes we think we are committed to something—when our actions indicate otherwise. Take out your calendar, your to-do list, and your bank statement. Determine how you spend your time and money. Commitment is often a case of "putting your money where your mouth is." If your statements and your actions don't match, no one will be convinced that you're committed, no matter the cause. And speaking of causes, take some time to determine what you most value. Another way of saying that: Know what you'd be willing to die for. If it came down to it, what in life would you not be able to stop doing, no matter what the consequences were?

Even though commitment is really only measured by action, a leader's words of commitment are still important. Not only do they communicate your resolve and challenge people to trust you; they also give you motivation to follow through because the commitment has been made public. If taking the first step toward commitment is a problem, try doing what Thomas Edison did. When he had a good idea for an invention, he would call a press conference to announce it. Then he'd go into his lab and make it happen.

Half-hearted leadership produces half-hearted followers. If you want your team to fight to win, you need to be willing to lead the charge.

# CASE STUDIES

Read these case studies from the Bible and answer the study questions that follow.

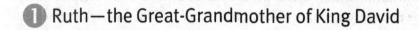 ## Ruth—the Great-Grandmother of King David

### Ruth 1:3–22

> ³ Now Elimelek, Naomi's husband, died, and she was left with her two sons.
> ⁴ They married Moabite women, one named Orpah and the other Ruth.
> After they had lived there about ten years, ⁵ both Mahlon and Kilion also died, and Naomi was left without her two sons and her husband.
>
> ⁶ When Naomi heard in Moab that the LORD had come to the aid of his people by providing food for them, she and her daughters-in-law prepared

to return home from there. ⁷ With her two daughters-in-law she left the place where she had been living and set out on the road that would take them back to the land of Judah.

⁸ Then Naomi said to her two daughters-in-law, "Go back, each of you, to your mother's home. May the LORD show you kindness, as you have shown kindness to your dead husbands and to me. ⁹ May the LORD grant that each of you will find rest in the home of another husband."

Then she kissed them goodbye and they wept aloud ¹⁰ and said to her, "We will go back with you to your people."

¹¹ But Naomi said, "Return home, my daughters. Why would you come with me? Am I going to have any more sons, who could become your husbands? ¹² Return home, my daughters; I am too old to have another husband. Even if I thought there was still hope for me—even if I had a husband tonight and then gave birth to sons— ¹³ would you wait until they grew up? Would you remain unmarried for them? No, my daughters. It is more bitter for me than for you, because the LORD's hand has turned against me!"

¹⁴ At this they wept aloud again. Then Orpah kissed her mother-in-law goodbye, but Ruth clung to her.

¹⁵ "Look," said Naomi, "your sister-in-law is going back to her people and her gods. Go back with her."

¹⁶ But Ruth replied, "Don't urge me to leave you or to turn back from you. Where you go I will go, and where you stay I will stay. Your people will be my people and your God my God. ¹⁷ Where you die I will die, and there I will be buried. May the LORD deal with me, be it ever so severely, if even death separates you and me." ¹⁸ When Naomi realized that Ruth was determined to go with her, she stopped urging her.

¹⁹ So the two women went on until they came to Bethlehem. When they arrived in Bethlehem, the whole town was stirred because of them, and the women exclaimed, "Can this be Naomi?"

²⁰ "Don't call me Naomi," she told them. "Call me Mara, because the Almighty has made my life very bitter. ²¹ I went away full, but the LORD has brought me back empty. Why call me Naomi? The LORD has afflicted me; the Almighty has brought misfortune upon me."

²² So Naomi returned from Moab accompanied by Ruth the Moabite, her daughter-in-law, arriving in Bethlehem as the barley harvest was beginning.

## Study Questions

1. What was Naomi's motivation for wanting to send Orpah and Ruth back home? Was that good or bad leadership?

_____

_____

_____

_____

2. Why do you think Orpah took her advice and Ruth didn't? Why do you think Ruth was devoted to her mother-in-law?

_____

_____

_____

_____

_____

3. Examine Ruth's reply to Naomi. Based on her statements, how would you rate her level of commitment? If Naomi had *ordered* her to go home, do you think Ruth would have obeyed? Explain.

_____

_____

_____

_____

## ② Caleb and Joshua Will Enter the Promised Land

### Numbers 14:1–24

[1] That night all the members of the community raised their voices and wept aloud. [2] All the Israelites grumbled against Moses and Aaron, and the whole assembly said to them, "If only we had died in Egypt! Or in this wilderness!

*³ Why is the LORD bringing us to this land only to let us fall by the sword? Our wives and children will be taken as plunder. Wouldn't it be better for us to go back to Egypt?" ⁴ And they said to each other, "We should choose a leader and go back to Egypt."*

*⁵ Then Moses and Aaron fell facedown in front of the whole Israelite assembly gathered there. ⁶ Joshua son of Nun and Caleb son of Jephunneh, who were among those who had explored the land, tore their clothes ⁷ and said to the entire Israelite assembly, "The land we passed through and explored is exceedingly good. ⁸ If the LORD is pleased with us, he will lead us into that land, a land flowing with milk and honey, and will give it to us. ⁹ Only do not rebel against the LORD. And do not be afraid of the people of the land, because we will devour them. Their protection is gone, but the LORD is with us. Do not be afraid of them."*

*¹⁰ But the whole assembly talked about stoning them. Then the glory of the LORD appeared at the tent of meeting to all the Israelites. ¹¹ The LORD said to Moses, "How long will these people treat me with contempt? How long will they refuse to believe in me, in spite of all the signs I have performed among them? ¹² I will strike them down with a plague and destroy them, but I will make you into a nation greater and stronger than they."*

*¹³ Moses said to the LORD, "Then the Egyptians will hear about it! By your power you brought these people up from among them. ¹⁴ And they will tell the inhabitants of this land about it. They have already heard that you, LORD, are with these people and that you, LORD, have been seen face to face, that your cloud stays over them, and that you go before them in a pillar of cloud by day and a pillar of fire by night. ¹⁵ If you put all these people to death, leaving none alive, the nations who have heard this report about you will say, ¹⁶ 'The LORD was not able to bring these people into the land he promised them on oath, so he slaughtered them in the wilderness.'*

*¹⁷ "Now may the Lord's strength be displayed, just as you have declared: ¹⁸ 'The LORD is slow to anger, abounding in love and forgiving sin and rebellion. Yet he does not leave the guilty unpunished; he punishes the children for the sin of the parents to the third and fourth generation.' ¹⁹ In accordance with your great love, forgive the sin of these people, just as you have pardoned them from the time they left Egypt until now."*

<sup>20</sup> The LORD replied, "I have forgiven them, as you asked. <sup>21</sup> Nevertheless, as surely as I live and as surely as the glory of the LORD fills the whole earth, <sup>22</sup> not one of those who saw my glory and the signs I performed in Egypt and in the wilderness but who disobeyed me and tested me ten times — <sup>23</sup> not one of them will ever see the land I promised on oath to their ancestors. No one who has treated me with contempt will ever see it. <sup>24</sup> But because my servant Caleb has a different spirit and follows me wholeheartedly, I will bring him into the land he went to, and his descendants will inherit it.

## Joshua 14:6–15

<sup>6</sup> Now the people of Judah approached Joshua at Gilgal, and Caleb son of Jephunneh the Kenizzite said to him, "You know what the LORD said to Moses the man of God at Kadesh Barnea about you and me. <sup>7</sup> I was forty years old when Moses the servant of the LORD sent me from Kadesh Barnea to explore the land. And I brought him back a report according to my convictions, <sup>8</sup> but my fellow Israelites who went up with me made the hearts of the people melt in fear. I, however, followed the LORD my God wholeheartedly. <sup>9</sup> So on that day Moses swore to me, 'The land on which your feet have walked will be your inheritance and that of your children forever, because you have followed the LORD my God wholeheartedly.'

<sup>10</sup> "Now then, just as the LORD promised, he has kept me alive for forty-five years since the time he said this to Moses, while Israel moved about in the wilderness. So here I am today, eighty-five years old! <sup>11</sup> I am still as strong today as the day Moses sent me out; I'm just as vigorous to go out to battle now as I was then. <sup>12</sup> Now give me this hill country that the LORD promised me that day. You yourself heard then that the Anakites were there and their cities were large and fortified, but, the LORD helping me, I will drive them out just as he said."

<sup>13</sup> Then Joshua blessed Caleb son of Jephunneh and gave him Hebron as his inheritance. <sup>14</sup> So Hebron has belonged to Caleb son of Jephunneh the Kenizzite ever since, because he followed the LORD, the God of Israel, wholeheartedly. <sup>15</sup> (Hebron used to be called Kiriath Arba after Arba, who was the greatest man among the Anakites.)

Then the land had rest from war.

## Study Questions

1. What separated Joshua and Caleb from the rest of the Israelites? Did those two men lack fear? Did the others lack faith? Explain your opinion.

_____

_____

_____

_____

_____

2. What role does conviction play in commitment?

_____

_____

_____

_____

_____

3. What do you think would have happened to the Israelites if they had not rebelled against God?

_____

_____

_____

_____

_____

4. What was Caleb's reward for his full commitment? What was Joshua's? What, if anything, do you believe God promises those who are committed to him and who wholeheartedly follow him?

_____

_____

_____

_____

_____

## 3 Stephen Pays a Price for Commitment

### Acts 6:8–15

*8 Now Stephen, a man full of God's grace and power, performed great wonders and signs among the people. 9 Opposition arose, however, from members of the Synagogue of the Freedmen (as it was called)—Jews of Cyrene and Alexandria as well as the provinces of Cilicia and Asia—who began to argue with Stephen. 10 But they could not stand up against the wisdom the Spirit gave him as he spoke.*

*12 Then they secretly persuaded some men to say, "We have heard Stephen speak blasphemous words against Moses and against God."*

*12 So they stirred up the people and the elders and the teachers of the law. They seized Stephen and brought him before the Sanhedrin. 13 They produced false witnesses, who testified, "This fellow never stops speaking against this holy place and against the law. 14 For we have heard him say that this Jesus of Nazareth will destroy this place and change the customs Moses handed down to us."*

*15 All who were sitting in the Sanhedrin looked intently at Stephen, and they saw that his face was like the face of an angel.*

### Acts 7:1–4, 8–10, 17–25, 29–39, 44–60

*1 Then the high priest asked Stephen, "Are these charges true?"*

*2 To this he replied: "Brothers and fathers, listen to me! The God of glory appeared to our father Abraham while he was still in Mesopotamia, before he lived in Harran. 3 'Leave your country and your people,' God said, 'and go to the land I will show you.'*

*4 "So he left the land of the Chaldeans and settled in Harran.... 8 Then he gave Abraham the covenant of circumcision. And Abraham became the father of Isaac and circumcised him eight days after his birth. Later Isaac became the father of Jacob, and Jacob became the father of the twelve patriarchs.*

*9 "Because the patriarchs were jealous of Joseph, they sold him as a slave into Egypt. But God was with him 10 and rescued him from all his troubles.*

*He gave Joseph wisdom and enabled him to gain the goodwill of Pharaoh king of Egypt. So Pharaoh made him ruler over Egypt and all his palace. . . .*

*[17] "As the time drew near for God to fulfill his promise to Abraham, the number of our people in Egypt had greatly increased. [18] Then 'a new king, to whom Joseph meant nothing, came to power in Egypt.' [19] He dealt treacherously with our people and oppressed our ancestors by forcing them to throw out their newborn babies so that they would die.*

*[20] "At that time Moses was born, and he was no ordinary child. For three months he was cared for by his family. [21] When he was placed outside, Pharaoh's daughter took him and brought him up as her own son. [22] Moses was educated in all the wisdom of the Egyptians and was powerful in speech and action.*

*[23] "When Moses was forty years old, he decided to visit his own people, the Israelites. [24] He saw one of them being mistreated by an Egyptian, so he went to his defense and avenged him by killing the Egyptian. [25] Moses thought that his own people would realize that God was using him to rescue them, but they did not. . . .*

*[29] He fled to Midian, where he settled as a foreigner and had two sons.*

*[30] "After forty years had passed, an angel appeared to Moses in the flames of a burning bush in the desert near Mount Sinai. [31] When he saw this, he was amazed at the sight. As he went over to get a closer look, he heard the Lord say: [32] 'I am the God of your fathers, the God of Abraham, Isaac and Jacob.' Moses trembled with fear and did not dare to look.*

*[33] "Then the Lord said to him, 'Take off your sandals, for the place where you are standing is holy ground. [34] I have indeed seen the oppression of my people in Egypt. I have heard their groaning and have come down to set them free. Now come, I will send you back to Egypt.'*

*[35] "This is the same Moses they had rejected with the words, 'Who made you ruler and judge?' He was sent to be their ruler and deliverer by God himself, through the angel who appeared to him in the bush. [36] He led them out of Egypt and performed wonders and signs in Egypt, at the Red Sea and for forty years in the wilderness.*

*[37] "This is the Moses who told the Israelites, 'God will raise up for you a prophet like me from your own people.' [38] He was in the assembly in the wilderness, with the angel who spoke to him on Mount Sinai, and with our ancestors; and he received living words to pass on to us.*

39 *"But our ancestors refused to obey him. Instead, they rejected him and in their hearts turned back to Egypt. . . .*

44 *"Our ancestors had the tabernacle of the covenant law with them in the wilderness. It had been made as God directed Moses, according to the pattern he had seen.* 45 *After receiving the tabernacle, our ancestors under Joshua brought it with them when they took the land from the nations God drove out before them. It remained in the land until the time of David,* 46 *who enjoyed God's favor and asked that he might provide a dwelling place for the God of Jacob.* 47 *But it was Solomon who built a house for him.*

48 *"However, the Most High does not live in houses made by human hands. As the prophet says:*

49 *" 'Heaven is my throne,*
*and the earth is my footstool.*
*What kind of house will you build for me?*
*says the Lord.*
*Or where will my resting place be?*
50 *Has not my hand made all these things?'*

51 *"You stiff-necked people! Your hearts and ears are still uncircumcised. You are just like your ancestors: You always resist the Holy Spirit!* 52 *Was there ever a prophet your ancestors did not persecute? They even killed those who predicted the coming of the Righteous One. And now you have betrayed and murdered him—* 53 *you who have received the law that was given through angels but have not obeyed it."*

54 *When the members of the Sanhedrin heard this, they were furious and gnashed their teeth at him.* 55 *But Stephen, full of the Holy Spirit, looked up to heaven and saw the glory of God, and Jesus standing at the right hand of God.* 56 *"Look," he said, "I see heaven open and the Son of Man standing at the right hand of God."*

57 *At this they covered their ears and, yelling at the top of their voices, they all rushed at him,* 58 *dragged him out of the city and began to stone him. Meanwhile, the witnesses laid their coats at the feet of a young man named Saul.*

59 *While they were stoning him, Stephen prayed, "Lord Jesus, receive my spirit."* 60 *Then he fell on his knees and cried out, "Lord, do not hold this sin against them." When he had said this, he fell asleep.*

## Study Questions

1. Why do you think Stephen summarized the history of Israel from Moses to
   the building of Solomon's temple as he addressed the people?

   _____

   _____

   _____

   _____

   _____

   _____

2. What do you think Stephen was hoping to accomplish when he criticized
   the members of the Sanhedrin?

   _____

   _____

   _____

   _____

   _____

   _____

   _____

3. Stephen is believed to be the first Christian martyr. Do you think he
   expected to be stoned to death for what he said? Do you think it would
   have made any difference? Would it have stopped him from speaking
   out? Explain.

   _____

   _____

   _____

   _____

   _____

   _____

# LEADERSHIP INSIGHT AND REFLECTION

Think about the many factors that may have come into play in the commitment of the people in the three passages: loyalty, responsibility, conviction, passion, purpose, faith, courage, and discipline. Which do you think were the strongest factors for each leader?

Ruth: _____

Caleb: _____

Joshua: _____

Stephen: _____

What factors come into play for you personally when it comes to commitment? How do they influence you?

_____

_____

_____

_____

_____

_____

_____

What factors *prevent* you from being fully committed?

_____

_____

_____

_____

How does any lack of commitment hinder your leadership and your success?

_____

_____

_____

_____

_____

# Taking Action

Where in your life is God asking you to step up to a higher level of commitment? Describe it here:

_____

_____

_____

_____

_____

_____

_____

What must you overcome to increase your commitment? What must you increase?

_____

_____

_____

_____

_____

_____

Describe what action you will take and when you will start.

_____

_____

_____

_____

_____

_____

_____

# GROUP DISCUSSION QUESTIONS

1. If you had been in Naomi's situation, would you have asked your daughters-in-law to accompany you to your home country, or would you have urged them to return to their families and try to find new husbands? Explain your answer.

2. What was the main cause of the Israelites' refusal to go into the promised land? Was it a failure of ability, courage, faith, leadership, or something else? Explain.

3. Could Moses, Joshua, or Caleb have forced the Israelites to cross over into the promised land? Why or why not? What do you think would have happened if they had tried?

4. What was your reaction when you read that Caleb was as strong and ready to do battle at age eighty-five as he had been at age forty? To what do you attribute that ability?

5. Stephen faced opposition for his commitment to follow Christ. Have you ever been criticized, opposed, or persecuted for your faith? If so, what happened? How did you handle it?

6. Which person or people did you most identify with from these passages: Naomi, Ruth, Orpah, Moses, Joshua, Caleb, or Stephen? Explain your answer.

7. How do you believe God is asking you to change to embody greater commitment as a leader? What do you intend to do, how will you do it, and when will you start?

# COMMUNICATION

## Without It You Travel Alone

## THE QUALITY DEFINED

Effective communication is key to every kind of relationship—whether with a spouse, a boss, a friend, an employee, or a colleague. We use it to express ideas, desires, and feelings. It can pull people together or push them apart. Without communication, it is impossible to connect with others. And those who do not connect travel through life alone. This is especially true in leadership.

You probably know this old saying: "He who thinks he leads, but has no one following, is only taking a walk." Every leader needs to possess the ability to communicate, because leadership only happens when we are able to influence people to follow us. People will not follow you if you can't help them understand what you want or where you are going.

Good leadership communication is clear, credible, and compelling. To improve in this area, it's important to be very clear about your message, and to express it as simply as possible. Focus not on impressing with big words or complex sentences. Instead, emphasize expressing your message with the best words for the job.

Effective communicators also know and understand their audience, and they think more about the audience than themselves. As you communicate with others—whether individuals or groups—ask yourself these questions: Who is my audience? What are their questions? What needs to be accomplished? And how much time do I have? People believe in great communicators because great communicators believe in people.

Credibility is also necessary to great communication. Followers need to be confident that you believe what you're saying and that your actions match it. There is no greater credibility than conviction in action. Finally, remember that the ultimate goal of communication is action. If you simply dump a bunch of information on people, you're not communicating. Every time you speak to people, give them something to feel, something to remember, and something to do. If you're successful in doing that, your ability to lead others will go to a whole new level.

# CASE STUDIES

Read these case studies from the Bible and answer the study questions that follow.

 ## The Decree of Darius

### Ezra 6:1–18

¹ *King Darius then issued an order, and they searched in the archives stored in the treasury at Babylon.* ² *A scroll was found in the citadel of Ecbatana in the province of Media, and this was written on it:*

*Memorandum:*
   ³ *In the first year of King Cyrus, the king issued a decree concerning the temple of God in Jerusalem:*
      *Let the temple be rebuilt as a place to present sacrifices, and let its foundations be laid. It is to be sixty cubits high and sixty cubits wide,* ⁴ *with three courses of large stones and one of timbers. The costs are to be paid by the royal treasury.* ⁵ *Also, the gold and silver articles of the house of God, which Nebuchadnezzar took from the temple in Jerusalem and brought to Babylon, are to be returned to their places in the temple in Jerusalem; they are to be deposited in the house of God.*

*⁶ Now then, Tattenai, governor of Trans-Euphrates, and Shethar-Bozenai and you other officials of that province, stay away from there. ⁷ Do not interfere with the work on this temple of God. Let the governor of the Jews and the Jewish elders rebuild this house of God on its site.*

*⁸ Moreover, I hereby decree what you are to do for these elders of the Jews in the construction of this house of God:*

*Their expenses are to be fully paid out of the royal treasury, from the revenues of Trans-Euphrates, so that the work will not stop. ⁹ Whatever is needed—young bulls, rams, male lambs for burnt offerings to the God of heaven, and wheat, salt, wine and olive oil, as requested by the priests in Jerusalem—must be given them daily without fail, ¹⁰ so that they may offer sacrifices pleasing to the God of heaven and pray for the well-being of the king and his sons.*

*¹¹ Furthermore, I decree that if anyone defies this edict, a beam is to be pulled from their house and they are to be impaled on it. And for this crime their house is to be made a pile of rubble. ¹² May God, who has caused his Name to dwell there, overthrow any king or people who lifts a hand to change this decree or to destroy this temple in Jerusalem.*

*I Darius have decreed it. Let it be carried out with diligence.*

*¹³ Then, because of the decree King Darius had sent, Tattenai, governor of Trans-Euphrates, and Shethar-Bozenai and their associates carried it out with diligence. ¹⁴ So the elders of the Jews continued to build and prosper under the preaching of Haggai the prophet and Zechariah, a descendant of Iddo. They finished building the temple according to the command of the God of Israel and the decrees of Cyrus, Darius and Artaxerxes, kings of Persia. ¹⁵ The temple was completed on the third day of the month Adar, in the sixth year of the reign of King Darius.*

*¹⁶ Then the people of Israel—the priests, the Levites and the rest of the exiles—celebrated the dedication of the house of God with joy. ¹⁷ For the dedication of this house of God they offered a hundred bulls, two hundred rams, four hundred male lambs and, as a sin offering for all Israel, twelve male goats, one for each of the tribes of Israel. ¹⁸ And they installed the priests in their divisions and the Levites in their groups for the service of God at Jerusalem, according to what is written in the Book of Moses.*

## Study Questions

1. Would you consider Darius' decree to be clear, credible, and compelling? Review the passage and list examples that exemplify these qualities.

_____

_____

_____

_____

_____

_____

2. Do you think Darius knew and understood his audience? Who were they, and how did Darius tailor his communication to them?

_____

_____

_____

_____

3. What was the goal of Darius' communication? Was it successful? Explain.

_____

_____

_____

_____

_____

## ② Jesus Models Clear Communication

### Matthew 22:23–40

_23 That same day the Sadducees, who say there is no resurrection, came to him with a question. 24 "Teacher," they said, "Moses told us that if a man_ *dies without having children, his brother must marry the widow and raise up offspring for him. ²⁵ Now there were seven brothers among us. The first one married and died, and since he had no children, he left his wife to his brother. ²⁶ The same thing happened to the second and third brother, right on down to the seventh. ²⁷ Finally, the woman died. ²⁸ Now then, at the resurrection, whose wife will she be of the seven, since all of them were married to her?"*

*²⁹ Jesus replied, "You are in error because you do not know the Scriptures or the power of God. ³⁰ At the resurrection people will neither marry nor be given in marriage; they will be like the angels in heaven. ³¹ But about the resurrection of the dead—have you not read what God said to you, ³² 'I am the God of Abraham, the God of Isaac, and the God of Jacob'? He is not the God of the dead but of the living."*

*³³ When the crowds heard this, they were astonished at his teaching.*

*³⁴ Hearing that Jesus had silenced the Sadducees, the Pharisees got together. ³⁵ One of them, an expert in the law, tested him with this question: ³⁶ "Teacher, which is the greatest commandment in the Law?"*

*³⁷ Jesus replied: "'Love the Lord your God with all your heart and with all your soul and with all your mind.' ³⁸ This is the first and greatest commandment. ³⁹ And the second is like it: 'Love your neighbor as yourself.' ⁴⁰ All the Law and the Prophets hang on these two commandments."*

## Study Questions

1. What was the motivation of the Sadducees and the Pharisees for questioning Jesus?

_____

_____

_____

_____

_____

2. The Sadducees, who were experts in the law, were silenced by Jesus' answer concerning the resurrection. The crowds, who were common people, were

astonished by Jesus' teaching. Judging by the reactions of these two groups, what observations can you make about Jesus' ability to communicate?

3. When Jesus said, "All the Law and the Prophets hang on these two commandments" (verse 40), what did he mean?

4. What do you think Jesus' ultimate goal was when he gave his answers to the Sadducees and Pharisees?

## ③ Paul Argues His Case

### Acts 26:1–32

---

[1] *Then Agrippa said to Paul, "You have permission to speak for yourself."*
*So Paul motioned with his hand and began his defense:* [2] *"King Agrippa, I consider myself fortunate to stand before you today as I make my defense*

against all the accusations of the Jews, [3] and especially so because you are well acquainted with all the Jewish customs and controversies. Therefore, I beg you to listen to me patiently.

[4] "The Jewish people all know the way I have lived ever since I was a child, from the beginning of my life in my own country, and also in Jerusalem. [5] They have known me for a long time and can testify, if they are willing, that I conformed to the strictest sect of our religion, living as a Pharisee. [6] And now it is because of my hope in what God has promised our ancestors that I am on trial today. [7] This is the promise our twelve tribes are hoping to see fulfilled as they earnestly serve God day and night. King Agrippa, it is because of this hope that these Jews are accusing me. [8] Why should any of you consider it incredible that God raises the dead?

[9] "I too was convinced that I ought to do all that was possible to oppose the name of Jesus of Nazareth. [10] And that is just what I did in Jerusalem. On the authority of the chief priests I put many of the Lord's people in prison, and when they were put to death, I cast my vote against them. [11] Many a time I went from one synagogue to another to have them punished, and I tried to force them to blaspheme. I was so obsessed with persecuting them that I even hunted them down in foreign cities.

[12] "On one of these journeys I was going to Damascus with the authority and commission of the chief priests. [13] About noon, King Agrippa, as I was on the road, I saw a light from heaven, brighter than the sun, blazing around me and my companions. [14] We all fell to the ground, and I heard a voice saying to me in Aramaic, 'Saul, Saul, why do you persecute me? It is hard for you to kick against the goads.'

[15] "Then I asked, 'Who are you, Lord?'

"'I am Jesus, whom you are persecuting,' the Lord replied. [16] 'Now get up and stand on your feet. I have appeared to you to appoint you as a servant and as a witness of what you have seen and will see of me. [17] I will rescue you from your own people and from the Gentiles. I am sending you to them [18] to open their eyes and turn them from darkness to light, and from the power of Satan to God, so that they may receive forgiveness of sins and a place among those who are sanctified by faith in me.'

[19] "So then, King Agrippa, I was not disobedient to the vision from heaven. [20] First to those in Damascus, then to those in Jerusalem and in all

*Judea, and then to the Gentiles, I preached that they should repent and turn to God and demonstrate their repentance by their deeds. ²¹ That is why some Jews seized me in the temple courts and tried to kill me. ²² But God has helped me to this very day; so I stand here and testify to small and great alike. I am saying nothing beyond what the prophets and Moses said would happen— ²³ that the Messiah would suffer and, as the first to rise from the dead, would bring the message of light to his own people and to the Gentiles."*

*²⁴ At this point Festus interrupted Paul's defense. "You are out of your mind, Paul!" he shouted. "Your great learning is driving you insane."*

*²⁵ "I am not insane, most excellent Festus," Paul replied. "What I am saying is true and reasonable. ²⁶ The king is familiar with these things, and I can speak freely to him. I am convinced that none of this has escaped his notice, because it was not done in a corner. ²⁷ King Agrippa, do you believe the prophets? I know you do."*

*²⁸ Then Agrippa said to Paul, "Do you think that in such a short time you can persuade me to be a Christian?"*

*²⁹ Paul replied, "Short time or long—I pray to God that not only you but all who are listening to me today may become what I am, except for these chains."*

*³⁰ The king rose, and with him the governor and Bernice and those sitting with them. ³¹ After they left the room, they began saying to one another, "This man is not doing anything that deserves death or imprisonment."*

*³² Agrippa said to Festus, "This man could have been set free if he had not appealed to Caesar."*

## Study Questions

1. What was Paul's communication strategy when speaking to Agrippa, Festus, and Bernice? Can you tell by examining what he said and how he said it?

_____

_____

_____

_____

_____

_____

2. What were Paul's motivations for making his defense to King Agrippa?

_____

_____

_____

_____

_____

_____

3. Where was Paul successful? Where wasn't he successful?

_____

_____

_____

_____

_____

_____

_____

4. What is the significance of Agrippa's statement to Festus, "This man could have been set free if he had not appealed to Caesar" (verse 32)?

_____

_____

_____

_____

_____

_____

_____

_____

_____

# LEADERSHIP INSIGHT AND REFLECTION

What is the role of authority in communication? Look at the three passages and analyze how it came into play for each of the communicators. For each of these communicators, were did their authority come from? And how did the people they addressed respond?

_____

_____

_____

_____

_____

_____

_____

_____

_____

_____

Where did their effectiveness come from? How much came from possessing authority, how much from understanding their audience, and how much from being clear, credible, and compelling?

_____

_____

_____

_____

_____

_____

_____

_____

_____

_____

_____

# TAKING ACTION

When you are communicating in a leadership role, how effective are you? Where are you falling short? Where do you most need to improve your authority, audience understanding, clarity, credibility, or passion?

_____

_____

_____

_____

_____

_____

_____

_____

_____

What do you need to change to improve your communication, and how will you go about doing it?

_____

_____

_____

_____

_____

_____

_____

_____

_____

_____

# GROUP DISCUSSION QUESTIONS

1. How carefully thought out and well-crafted do you think Darius' decree was? Explain your answer.

2. The Sadducees and Pharisees tried to put Jesus on the spot, yet he answered their questions expertly. How do you usually respond when people put you on the spot?

3. The New Testament contains examples of Paul's verbal communication, such as his address to Agrippa, as well as many letters he wrote. How important were these skills to Paul? What impact did they have?

4. What role does communication play in the life of a leader—in writing, one-on-one, and to an audience?

5. How would you rate yourself as a communicator on a scale of 1 (low) to 10 (high)? In which are you better: speaking or writing? Why?

6. Where do you most need to grow as a communicator? How would growing in this area help you as a leader?

7. What one thing could you do right now to most improve your effectiveness as a communicator? What action will you take to begin improving immediately?

# LESSON 5

# COMPETENCE

## If You Build It, They Will Come

### THE QUALITY DEFINED

Competence goes beyond words. It's the leader's ability to say it, plan it, and do it in such a way that others know that you know how—and are inspired to follow. We all admire people who display high competence, whether they are precision craftsmen, world-class athletes, or successful business leaders. But the truth is that you don't have to be Fabergé, LeBron James, or Bill Gates to excel in the area of competence.

If you want to cultivate competence, the first thing you need to do is show up. Responsible people show up when they're expected. But highly competent people take it a step further. They don't show up in body only. They come ready to play every day—no matter how they feel, what kind of circumstances they're facing, or how difficult they expect the game to be. All highly competent people also continually search for ways to keep learning, growing, and improving. They follow through with excellence. This is always a choice, an act of the will. As leaders, we expect our people to follow through when we hand them the ball. They expect us as leaders to follow through too, plus a whole lot more.

Highly competent leaders accomplish more than others expect. They always go the extra mile. For them, good enough is never good enough. This attitude within them inspires and motivates their people to do the same. While some people rely on relational skills alone to survive, effective leaders combine those skills with high competence to take their organization to new levels of excellence and influence.

# CASE STUDIES

Read these case studies from the Bible and answer the study questions that follow.

## ① Abraham's Obedience with Isaac

### Genesis 22:1–18

*¹ Some time later God tested Abraham. He said to him, "Abraham!"*

*"Here I am," he replied.*

*² Then God said, "Take your son, your only son, whom you love — Isaac — and go to the region of Moriah. Sacrifice him there as a burnt offering on a mountain I will show you."*

*³ Early the next morning Abraham got up and loaded his donkey. He took with him two of his servants and his son Isaac. When he had cut enough wood for the burnt offering, he set out for the place God had told him about. ⁴ On the third day Abraham looked up and saw the place in the distance. ⁵ He said to his servants, "Stay here with the donkey while I and the boy go over there. We will worship and then we will come back to you."*

*⁶ Abraham took the wood for the burnt offering and placed it on his son Isaac, and he himself carried the fire and the knife. As the two of them went on together, ⁷ Isaac spoke up and said to his father Abraham, "Father?"*

*"Yes, my son?" Abraham replied.*

*"The fire and wood are here," Isaac said, "but where is the lamb for the burnt offering?"*

*⁸ Abraham answered, "God himself will provide the lamb for the burnt offering, my son." And the two of them went on together.*

*⁹ When they reached the place God had told him about, Abraham built an altar there and arranged the wood on it. He bound his son Isaac and laid him on the altar, on top of the wood. ¹⁰ Then he reached out his hand and took* the knife to slay his son. <sup>11</sup> But the angel of the LORD called out to him from heaven, *"Abraham! Abraham!"*

*"Here I am,"* he replied.

<sup>12</sup> *"Do not lay a hand on the boy,"* he said. *"Do not do anything to him. Now I know that you fear God, because you have not withheld from me your son, your only son."*

<sup>13</sup> Abraham looked up and there in a thicket he saw a ram caught by its horns. He went over and took the ram and sacrificed it as a burnt offering instead of his son. <sup>14</sup> So Abraham called that place The LORD Will Provide. And to this day it is said, *"On the mountain of the LORD it will be provided."*

<sup>15</sup> The angel of the LORD called to Abraham from heaven a second time <sup>16</sup> and said, *"I swear by myself, declares the LORD, that because you have done this and have not withheld your son, your only son, <sup>17</sup> I will surely bless you and make your descendants as numerous as the stars in the sky and as the sand on the seashore. Your descendants will take possession of the cities of their enemies, <sup>18</sup> and through your offspring all nations on earth will be blessed, because you have obeyed me."*

## Study Questions

1. In what ways would you consider Abraham to have displayed competence? List the evidence you find in the passage.

2. If you had been asked by God to sacrifice someone you loved or something you valued highly, would you have fulfilled the task as competently as Abraham did? Explain how you think you would have handled it.

3. What were the underlying traits and motivations that enabled Abraham to act with competence in such a stressful situation?

_____

_____

_____

4. What do you draw upon when you need to be competent under duress?

_____

_____

_____

_____

## ❷ Hezekiah Becomes King of Judah

### 2 Chronicles 29:1–11, 15–36

*¹ Hezekiah was twenty-five years old when he became king, and he reigned in Jerusalem twenty-nine years. His mother's name was Abijah daughter of Zechariah. ² He did what was right in the eyes of the LORD, just as his father David had done.*

*³ In the first month of the first year of his reign, he opened the doors of the temple of the LORD and repaired them. ⁴ He brought in the priests and the Levites, assembled them in the square on the east side ⁵ and said: "Listen to me, Levites! Consecrate yourselves now and consecrate the temple of the LORD, the God of your ancestors. Remove all defilement from the sanctuary. ⁶ Our parents were unfaithful; they did evil in the eyes of the LORD our God and forsook him. They turned their faces away from the LORD's dwelling place and turned their backs on him. ⁷ They also shut the doors of the portico and put out the lamps. They did not burn incense or present any burnt offerings at the sanctuary to the God of Israel. ⁸ Therefore, the* anger of the LORD has fallen on Judah and Jerusalem; he has made them an object of dread and horror and scorn, as you can see with your own eyes. *9* This is why our fathers have fallen by the sword and why our sons and daughters and our wives are in captivity. *10* Now I intend to make a covenant with the LORD, the God of Israel, so that his fierce anger will turn away from us. *11* My sons, do not be negligent now, for the LORD has chosen you to stand before him and serve him, to minister before him and to burn incense." . . .

*15* When they had assembled their fellow Levites and consecrated themselves, they went in to purify the temple of the LORD, as the king had ordered, following the word of the LORD. *16* The priests went into the sanctuary of the LORD to purify it. They brought out to the courtyard of the LORD's temple everything unclean that they found in the temple of the LORD. The Levites took it and carried it out to the Kidron Valley. *17* They began the consecration on the first day of the first month, and by the eighth day of the month they reached the portico of the LORD. For eight more days they consecrated the temple of the LORD itself, finishing on the sixteenth day of the first month.

*18* Then they went in to King Hezekiah and reported: "We have purified the entire temple of the LORD, the altar of burnt offering with all its utensils, and the table for setting out the consecrated bread, with all its articles. *19* We have prepared and consecrated all the articles that King Ahaz removed in his unfaithfulness while he was king. They are now in front of the LORD's altar."

*20* Early the next morning King Hezekiah gathered the city officials together and went up to the temple of the LORD. *21* They brought seven bulls, seven rams, seven male lambs and seven male goats as a sin offering for the kingdom, for the sanctuary and for Judah. The king commanded the priests, the descendants of Aaron, to offer these on the altar of the LORD. *22* So they slaughtered the bulls, and the priests took the blood and splashed it against the altar; next they slaughtered the rams and splashed their blood against the altar; then they slaughtered the lambs and splashed their blood against the altar. *23* The goats for the sin offering were brought before the king and the assembly, and they laid their hands on them. *24* The priests then slaughtered the goats and presented their blood on the altar for a sin offering to atone for all Israel, because the king had ordered the burnt offering and the sin offering for all Israel.

[25] He stationed the Levites in the temple of the LORD with cymbals, harps and lyres in the way prescribed by David and Gad the king's seer and Nathan the prophet; this was commanded by the LORD through his prophets. [26] So the Levites stood ready with David's instruments, and the priests with their trumpets.

[27] Hezekiah gave the order to sacrifice the burnt offering on the altar. As the offering began, singing to the LORD began also, accompanied by trumpets and the instruments of David king of Israel. [28] The whole assembly bowed in worship, while the musicians played and the trumpets sounded. All this continued until the sacrifice of the burnt offering was completed.

[29] When the offerings were finished, the king and everyone present with him knelt down and worshiped. [30] King Hezekiah and his officials ordered the Levites to praise the LORD with the words of David and of Asaph the seer. So they sang praises with gladness and bowed down and worshiped.

[31] Then Hezekiah said, "You have now dedicated yourselves to the LORD. Come and bring sacrifices and thank offerings to the temple of the LORD." So the assembly brought sacrifices and thank offerings, and all whose hearts were willing brought burnt offerings.

[32] The number of burnt offerings the assembly brought was seventy bulls, a hundred rams and two hundred male lambs—all of them for burnt offerings to the LORD. [33] The animals consecrated as sacrifices amounted to six hundred bulls and three thousand sheep and goats. [34] The priests, however, were too few to skin all the burnt offerings; so their relatives the Levites helped them until the task was finished and until other priests had been consecrated, for the Levites had been more conscientious in consecrating themselves than the priests had been. [35] There were burnt offerings in abundance, together with the fat of the fellowship offerings and the drink offerings that accompanied the burnt offerings.

So the service of the temple of the LORD was reestablished. [36] Hezekiah and all the people rejoiced at what God had brought about for his people, because it was done so quickly.

## 2 Chronicles 31:20–21

*²⁰ This is what Hezekiah did throughout Judah, doing what was good and right and faithful before the Lᴏʀᴅ his God. ²¹ In everything that he undertook in the service of God's temple and in obedience to the law and the commands, he sought his God and worked wholeheartedly. And so he prospered.*

## Study Questions

1. At what point in his reign did Hezekiah initiate his actions related to the restoration of the Temple? What significance does that timing hold?

_____

_____

_____

_____

2. How much would the priests and the Levites have known about Hezekiah at that time? Why do you think they followed him?

_____

_____

_____

_____

_____

_____

3. What evidence do you see of Hezekiah's competence as a leader?

_____

_____

_____

_____

_____

4. What benefits of competence did Hezekiah receive personally? What benefits did the people receive? How did it impact the people of Judah?

_____

_____

_____

_____

_____

_____

_____

## ❸ The Qualifications for Overseers and Deacons

### 1 Timothy 3:1–13

*¹ Here is a trustworthy saying: Whoever aspires to be an overseer desires a noble task. ² Now the overseer is to be above reproach, faithful to his wife, temperate, self-controlled, respectable, hospitable, able to teach, ³ not given to drunkenness, not violent but gentle, not quarrelsome, not a lover of money. ⁴ He must manage his own family well and see that his children obey him, and he must do so in a manner worthy of full respect. ⁵ (If anyone does not know how to manage his own family, how can he take care of God's church?) ⁶ He must not be a recent convert, or he may become conceited and fall under the same judgment as the devil. ⁷ He must also have a good reputation with outsiders, so that he will not fall into disgrace and into the devil's trap.*

*⁸ In the same way, deacons are to be worthy of respect, sincere, not indulging in much wine, and not pursuing dishonest gain. ⁹ They must keep hold of the deep truths of the faith with a clear conscience. ¹⁰ They must first be tested; and then if there is nothing against them, let them serve as deacons.*

*¹¹ In the same way, the women are to be worthy of respect, not malicious talkers but temperate and trustworthy in everything.*

*¹² A deacon must be faithful to his wife and must manage his children and his household well. ¹³ Those who have served well gain an excellent standing and great assurance in their faith in Christ Jesus.*

## Study Questions

1. Which of the qualifications listed for church leaders are related to competence, and which are related to character?

   _____

   _____

   _____

   _____

   _____

   _____

   _____

2. Can a person possess good character and not be competent? Can someone be competent without having good character? What usually happens in each of these instances?

   _____

   _____

   _____

   _____

   _____

   _____

   _____

3. Why is it essential for a good leader to possess both qualities?

   _____

   _____

   _____

   _____

   _____

   _____

   _____

# LEADERSHIP INSIGHT AND REFLECTION

How much of competence can be attributed to intentionality and how much to skill? How do these two factors come into play in the first two biblical passages?

_____

_____

_____

_____

_____

_____

_____

_____

Which of those two traits comes more easily to you: skill or intentionality? Which is the greater strength? How do you cultivate each?

_____

_____

_____

_____

_____

# TAKING ACTION

What action is God wanting you to take to increase your competence? Is it a step toward better character, stronger skill, or greater intentionality?

_____

_____

_____

_____

_____

_____

**What exactly will you do to begin improving starting today?**

_____

_____

_____

_____

_____

_____

_____

_____

_____

_____

_____

_____

# GROUP DISCUSSION QUESTIONS

1. Abraham was focused enough on the task God gave him to do that he followed through quickly, yet he was open enough to God that he was stopped from actually killing Isaac. How do you think he was able to maintain this balance? How are you at keeping that balance?

2. Could Hezekiah have completed the task of repairing the temple without the priests and Levites? Could they have completed it without Hezekiah? What did each bring to the process?

3. The passage you read from 1 Timothy 3:1–13 describes qualifications for church leaders. How much would those qualifications apply to leaders outside of the church? How much do qualifications for leadership vary from setting to setting?

4. Which is the greater factor in success: the competence of the leader or of the people carrying out the objective to completion? Explain your answer.

5. When you first encounter a leader, what qualities do you look for? How high does competence rate on your list? Explain.

6. What was your greatest takeaway about competence in leadership from this lesson?

7. What action do you believe God is asking you to take in your leadership growth as a result of this lesson? When and how will you do it?

# COURAGE

## One Person with Courage Is a Majority

## THE QUALITY DEFINED

When we think of courage, we imagine someone taking action regardless of any risk involved. Whether they're standing up for an unpopular opinion, or making a frightening decision, or risking their life, we often picture them doing it fearlessly. But while all of those actions can demonstrate courage, they rarely demonstrate fearlessness. That's because courage means taking a risk *in spite of* fear, not in the absence of it.

Courageous leaders look fear in the face and decide to act on behalf of others anyway. They take the big risk and put their leadership on the line for the organization or team. As a result, they do great things. Courage is easy to see in war heroes, but it's also present in every great leader in business, government, and the church. Whenever you see significant progress in an organization, it's because the leader made courageous decisions.

What's ironic is that those who don't have the courage to take risks and those who do often experience the same amount of fear in life. Letting fear win limits a leader. The Roman historian Tacitus said, "The desire for safety stands against every great and noble enterprise." But taking action with courage has the opposite effect. It opens doors, and that's one of its most wonderful benefits. It also inspires followers. Courage demonstrated by any person encourages others. But courage in a leader inspires them. It makes people want to follow them. "Courage is contagious," said evangelist Billy Graham. "When a brave man takes a stand, the spines of others are stiffened."

Eleanor Roosevelt said, "You gain strength, courage, and confidence by every experience in which you really stop to look fear in the face. You are able to say to yourself, 'I lived through this horror. I can take the next thing that comes along.' You must do the thing you think you cannot do." Leaders who face their fears and step out of their comfort zone on a regular basis impart their courage to their followers. And the entire team or organization is empowered to take big risks, make frightening decisions, and do great things.

# CASE STUDIES

Read these case studies from the Bible and answer the study questions that follow.

## ❶ Joshua Leads the People Across the Jordan

### Joshua 1:1–11

¹ *After the death of Moses the servant of the LORD, the LORD said to Joshua son of Nun, Moses' aide:* ² *"Moses my servant is dead. Now then, you and all these people, get ready to cross the Jordan River into the land I am about to give to them—to the Israelites.* ³ *I will give you every place where you set your foot, as I promised Moses.* ⁴ *Your territory will extend from the desert to Lebanon, and from the great river, the Euphrates—all the Hittite country—to the Mediterranean Sea in the west.* ⁵ *No one will be able to stand against you all the days of your life. As I was with Moses, so I will be with you; I will never leave you nor forsake you.* ⁶ *Be strong and courageous, because you will lead these people to inherit the land I swore to their ancestors to give them.*

*7 "Be strong and very courageous. Be careful to obey all the law my
servant Moses gave you; do not turn from it to the right or to the left,
that you may be successful wherever you go. 8 Keep this Book of the Law
always on your lips; meditate on it day and night, so that you may be
careful to do everything written in it. Then you will be prosperous and
successful. 9 Have I not commanded you? Be strong and courageous.
Do not be afraid; do not be discouraged, for the LORD your God will be
with you wherever you go."*

*10 So Joshua ordered the officers of the people: 11 "Go through the
camp and tell the people, 'Get your provisions ready. Three days from
now you will cross the Jordan here to go in and take possession of the
land the LORD your God is giving you for your own.'"*

## Joshua 3:1–4, 14–17

*1 Early in the morning Joshua and all the Israelites set out from Shittim
and went to the Jordan, where they camped before crossing over. 2 After
three days the officers went throughout the camp, 3 giving orders to the
people: "When you see the ark of the covenant of the LORD your God, and
the Levitical priests carrying it, you are to move out from your positions
and follow it. 4 Then you will know which way to go, since you have never
been this way before." . . .*

*14 So when the people broke camp to cross the Jordan, the priests
carrying the ark of the covenant went ahead of them. 15 Now the Jordan
is at flood stage all during harvest. Yet as soon as the priests who
carried the ark reached the Jordan and their feet touched the water's
edge, 16 the water from upstream stopped flowing. It piled up in a heap
a great distance away, at a town called Adam in the vicinity of Zarethan,
while the water flowing down to the Sea of the Arabah (that is, the
Dead Sea) was completely cut off. So the people crossed over opposite
Jericho. 17 The priests who carried the ark of the covenant of the
LORD stopped in the middle of the Jordan and stood on dry ground,
while all Israel passed by until the whole nation had completed the
crossing on dry ground.*

## Study Questions

1. Joshua, along with Caleb, had seen the promised land before. The first time God directed the Israelites to cross over the Jordan and take it forty years before, Joshua had been one of the spies. But the people had refused. How do you think Joshua felt about what God was telling him to do this time?

_____

_____

_____

_____

2. How many times in this short passage did the Lord tell Joshua to be strong and courageous? Why do you think he repeated this phrase? What things might Joshua have been afraid of?

_____

_____

_____

_____

3. What is the significance of the phrase, "Since you have never been this way before" (3:4)? What impact would that fact have on the Israelites? What impact on Joshua?

_____

_____

_____

_____

4. Could this generation of Israelites have rebelled the way the previous generation did? If so, what do you think God would have done?

_____

_____

_____

_____

## ② Elijah on Mount Carmel

### 1 Kings 18:16–40

*¹⁶ So Obadiah went to meet Ahab and told him, and Ahab went to meet Elijah. ¹⁷ When he saw Elijah, he said to him, "Is that you, you troubler of Israel?"*

*¹⁸ "I have not made trouble for Israel," Elijah replied. "But you and your father's family have. You have abandoned the LORD's commands and have followed the Baals. ¹⁹ Now summon the people from all over Israel to meet me on Mount Carmel. And bring the four hundred and fifty prophets of Baal and the four hundred prophets of Asherah, who eat at Jezebel's table."*

*²⁰ So Ahab sent word throughout all Israel and assembled the prophets on Mount Carmel. ²¹ Elijah went before the people and said, "How long will you waver between two opinions? If the LORD is God, follow him; but if Baal is God, follow him."*

*But the people said nothing.*

*²² Then Elijah said to them, "I am the only one of the LORD's prophets left, but Baal has four hundred and fifty prophets. ²³ Get two bulls for us. Let Baal's prophets choose one for themselves, and let them cut it into pieces and put it on the wood but not set fire to it. I will prepare the other bull and put it on the wood but not set fire to it. ²⁴ Then you call on the name of your god, and I will call on the name of the LORD. The god who answers by fire—he is God."*

*Then all the people said, "What you say is good."*

*²⁵ Elijah said to the prophets of Baal, "Choose one of the bulls and prepare it first, since there are so many of you. Call on the name of your god, but do not light the fire." ²⁶ So they took the bull given them and prepared it.*

*Then they called on the name of Baal from morning till noon. "Baal, answer us!" they shouted. But there was no response; no one answered. And they danced around the altar they had made.*

*²⁷ At noon Elijah began to taunt them. "Shout louder!" he said. "Surely he is a god! Perhaps he is deep in thought, or busy, or traveling. Maybe he is sleeping and must be awakened." ²⁸ So they shouted louder and slashed themselves with swords and spears, as was their custom, until their blood flowed. ²⁹ Midday passed, and they continued their frantic prophesying* until the time for the evening sacrifice. But there was no response, no one answered, no one paid attention.

*30* Then Elijah said to all the people, "Come here to me." They came to him, and he repaired the altar of the LORD, which had been torn down. *31* Elijah took twelve stones, one for each of the tribes descended from Jacob, to whom the word of the LORD had come, saying, "Your name shall be Israel." *32* With the stones he built an altar in the name of the LORD, and he dug a trench around it large enough to hold two seahs of seed. *33* He arranged the wood, cut the bull into pieces and laid it on the wood. Then he said to them, "Fill four large jars with water and pour it on the offering and on the wood."

*34* "Do it again," he said, and they did it again.

"Do it a third time," he ordered, and they did it the third time. *35* The water ran down around the altar and even filled the trench.

*36* At the time of sacrifice, the prophet Elijah stepped forward and prayed: "LORD, the God of Abraham, Isaac and Israel, let it be known today that you are God in Israel and that I am your servant and have done all these things at your command. *37* Answer me, LORD, answer me, so these people will know that you, LORD, are God, and that you are turning their hearts back again."

*38* Then the fire of the LORD fell and burned up the sacrifice, the wood, the stones and the soil, and also licked up the water in the trench.

*39* When all the people saw this, they fell prostrate and cried, "The LORD— he is God! The LORD—he is God!"

*40* Then Elijah commanded them, "Seize the prophets of Baal. Don't let anyone get away!" They seized them, and Elijah had them brought down to the Kishon Valley and slaughtered there.

## Study Questions

1. Elijah said that he acted in accordance with God's command, but even knowing this, how much courage did it take for him to call for a showdown between him and the four hundred and fifty prophets of Baal?

2. What do you think would have happened to Elijah if God had not answered his prayer and sent down fire to consume the sacrifice?

_____

_____

_____

_____

_____

3. Why was something this dramatic needed to get the Israelites to recognize God and follow him? What does this incident teach about leadership?

_____

_____

_____

_____

_____

## ❸ Esther's Courage to Rescue Her People

### Esther 3:8–11

*8 Then Haman said to King Xerxes, "There is a certain people dispersed among the peoples in all the provinces of your kingdom who keep themselves separate. Their customs are different from those of all other people, and they do not obey the king's laws; it is not in the king's best interest to tolerate them. 9 If it pleases the king, let a decree be issued to destroy them, and I will give ten thousand talents of silver to the king's administrators for the royal treasury."*

*10 So the king took his signet ring from his finger and gave it to Haman son of Hammedatha, the Agagite, the enemy of the Jews. 11 "Keep the money," the king said to Haman, "and do with the people as you please."*

## Esther 4:1, 4–7, 9–13, 15–16

*¹ When Mordecai learned of all that had been done, he tore his clothes, put on sackcloth and ashes, and went out into the city, wailing loudly and bitterly. . . .*

*⁴ When Esther's eunuchs and female attendants came and told her about Mordecai, she was in great distress. She sent clothes for him to put on instead of his sackcloth, but he would not accept them. ⁵ Then Esther summoned Hathak, one of the king's eunuchs assigned to attend her, and ordered him to find out what was troubling Mordecai and why.*

*⁶ So Hathak went out to Mordecai in the open square of the city in front of the king's gate. ⁷ Mordecai told him everything that had happened to him, including the exact amount of money Haman had promised to pay into the royal treasury for the destruction of the Jews. . . .*

*⁹ Hathak went back and reported to Esther what Mordecai had said. ¹⁰ Then she instructed him to say to Mordecai, ¹¹ "All the king's officials and the people of the royal provinces know that for any man or woman who approaches the king in the inner court without being summoned the king has but one law: that they be put to death unless the king extends the gold scepter to them and spares their lives. But thirty days have passed since I was called to go to the king."*

*¹² When Esther's words were reported to Mordecai, ¹³ he sent back this answer: "Do not think that because you are in the king's house you alone of all the Jews will escape. . . .*

*¹⁵ Then Esther sent this reply to Mordecai: . . . ¹⁶ "I will go to the king, even though it is against the law. And if I perish, I perish."*

## Esther 5:1–3

*¹ On the third day Esther put on her royal robes and stood in the inner court of the palace, in front of the king's hall. The king was sitting on his royal throne in the hall, facing the entrance. ² When he saw Queen Esther standing in the court, he was pleased with her and held out to her the gold scepter that was in his hand. So Esther approached and touched the tip of the scepter.*

*³ Then the king asked, "What is it, Queen Esther? What is your request? Even up to half the kingdom, it will be given you."*

## Esther 7:3–10

³ Then Queen Esther answered, "If I have found favor with you, Your Majesty, and if it pleases you, grant me my life—this is my petition. And spare my people—this is my request. ⁴ For I and my people have been sold to be destroyed, killed and annihilated. If we had merely been sold as male and female slaves, I would have kept quiet, because no such distress would justify disturbing the king."

⁵ King Xerxes asked Queen Esther, "Who is he? Where is he—the man who has dared to do such a thing?"

⁶ Esther said, "An adversary and enemy! This vile Haman!"

Then Haman was terrified before the king and queen. ⁷ The king got up in a rage, left his wine and went out into the palace garden. But Haman, realizing that the king had already decided his fate, stayed behind to beg Queen Esther for his life.

⁸ Just as the king returned from the palace garden to the banquet hall, Haman was falling on the couch where Esther was reclining.

The king exclaimed, "Will he even molest the queen while she is with me in the house?"

As soon as the word left the king's mouth, they covered Haman's face. ⁹ Then Harbona, one of the eunuchs attending the king, said, "A pole reaching to a height of fifty cubits stands by Haman's house. He had it set up for Mordecai, who spoke up to help the king."

The king said, "Impale him on it!" ¹⁰ So they impaled Haman on the pole he had set up for Mordecai. Then the king's fury subsided.

## Study Questions

1. What does it say about the leadership culture of Persia that anyone who approached the king without being summoned would be executed unless the king gave a sign to do otherwise?

   _____

   _____

   _____

   _____

2. Why do you think Esther delayed communicating her request to king Xerxes?

_____

_____

_____

_____

_____


3. The action Esther took was in response to a request from her uncle Mordecai, not a command from God. How do you think that affected her?

_____

_____

_____

_____

# LEADERSHIP INSIGHT AND REFLECTION

Think about the three passages. What was at stake for each leader and the people involved?

_____

_____

_____

_____

_____

_____

_____

How much courage did it take for each of the leaders to take action? In Joshua and Elijah's case, God had commanded them to do what they did; but in Esther's case, he had not. What could have gone wrong?

_____

_____

_____

_____

How do you know when to take courageous action as a leader? What principles or factors inform your decision making?

_____

_____

_____

_____

_____

_____

# TAKING ACTION

Think about your current leadership role and how you would be able to help the people you lead. What courageous action is God asking you to take as a leader? Describe it.

_____

_____

_____

_____

_____

**What can you do to become strong and courageous?**

_____

_____

_____

_____

_____

**When will you take action?**

_____

_____

_____

_____

_____

# GROUP DISCUSSION QUESTIONS

1. Who was the greater leader: Moses, who led the Israelites out of Egypt, or Joshua, who led the Israelites into the promised land? Explain your answer.

2. What was your reaction when you read how God responded to Elijah's request on Mount Carmel by burning up the sacrifice, the water, and even the stones? What was your reaction when he directed all the prophets of Baal to be slaughtered? Why do you think he did that?

3. What assurance did Esther have that God would rescue her and her people?

4. Which leader in the passages do you relate to most? Why?

5. In what kinds of situations do you most often respond with courage and in which do you have a difficult time? Why do you think that is?

6. What is the role of courage in leading others?

7. What courageous action do you believe God is asking you to take in your leadership? When and how will you do it?

# LESSON 7

# DISCERNMENT

## Put an End to Unsolved Mysteries

## THE QUALITY DEFINED

Simply stated, discernment is the ability to find the root of the matter, to read between the lines and see beneath the surface of a situation. It's more than a logical understanding of the facts; it also relies on experience and the wisdom and intuition that comes from it. Discernment is critical for effective leadership, because leaders face complex decisions every day, and they can rarely gather all of the information that would be needed to decide with 100 percent certainty. Researcher Henry Mintzberg of McGill University said, "Organizational effectiveness does not lie in that narrowminded concept called rationality. It lies in the blend of clearheaded logic and powerful intuition." Discernment enables a leader to see a partial picture, fill in the missing pieces intuitively, and make a good decision.

So how does a leader develop discernment? First, place high value on non-traditional thinking and embrace change, ambiguity, and uncertainty. Learn from wise and discerning leaders that you admire. Also get in the habit of evaluating your own past experience. Maximize the learning that can come from living life. Examine past decisions. Where did logic serve you? What instincts did you follow that helped? As you evaluate many decisions, look for patterns. Most people have one area—usually in the area of their gifting—where they have the best instincts. By capitalizing on those excellent instincts, they can continue to use and refine them.

# CASE STUDIES

Read these case studies from the Bible and answer the study questions that follow.

## ① Pharaoh Recognizes Joseph's Wisdom

### Genesis 41:25–57

*25 Then Joseph said to Pharaoh, "The dreams of Pharaoh are one and the same. God has revealed to Pharaoh what he is about to do.*
*26 The seven good cows are seven years, and the seven good heads of grain are seven years; it is one and the same dream. 27 The seven lean, ugly cows that came up afterward are seven years, and so are the seven worthless heads of grain scorched by the east wind: They are seven years of famine.*
 *28 "It is just as I said to Pharaoh: God has shown Pharaoh what he is about to do. 29 Seven years of great abundance are coming throughout the land of Egypt, 30 but seven years of famine will follow them. Then all the abundance in Egypt will be forgotten, and the famine will ravage the land. 31 The abundance in the land will not be remembered, because the famine that follows it will be so severe. 32 The reason the dream was given to Pharaoh in two forms is that the matter has been firmly decided by God, and God will do it soon.*
 *33 "And now let Pharaoh look for a discerning and wise man and put him in charge of the land of Egypt. 34 Let Pharaoh appoint commissioners over the land to take a fifth of the harvest of Egypt during the seven years of abundance. 35 They should collect all the food of these good years that are coming and store up the grain under the authority of Pharaoh, to be kept in the cities for food. 36 This food should be held in reserve for*

the country, to be used during the seven years of famine that will come upon Egypt, so that the country may not be ruined by the famine."

37 The plan seemed good to Pharaoh and to all his officials. 38 So Pharaoh asked them, "Can we find anyone like this man, one in whom is the spirit of God?"

39 Then Pharaoh said to Joseph, "Since God has made all this known to you, there is no one so discerning and wise as you. 40 You shall be in charge of my palace, and all my people are to submit to your orders. Only with respect to the throne will I be greater than you."

41 So Pharaoh said to Joseph, "I hereby put you in charge of the whole land of Egypt." 42 Then Pharaoh took his signet ring from his finger and put it on Joseph's finger. He dressed him in robes of fine linen and put a gold chain around his neck. 43 He had him ride in a chariot as his second-in-command, and people shouted before him, "Make way!" Thus he put him in charge of the whole land of Egypt.

44 Then Pharaoh said to Joseph, "I am Pharaoh, but without your word no one will lift hand or foot in all Egypt." 45 Pharaoh gave Joseph the name Zaphenath-Paneah and gave him Asenath daughter of Potiphera, priest of On, to be his wife. And Joseph went throughout the land of Egypt.

46 Joseph was thirty years old when he entered the service of Pharaoh king of Egypt. And Joseph went out from Pharaoh's presence and traveled throughout Egypt. 47 During the seven years of abundance the land produced plentifully. 48 Joseph collected all the food produced in those seven years of abundance in Egypt and stored it in the cities. In each city he put the food grown in the fields surrounding it. 49 Joseph stored up huge quantities of grain, like the sand of the sea; it was so much that he stopped keeping records because it was beyond measure.

50 Before the years of famine came, two sons were born to Joseph by Asenath daughter of Potiphera, priest of On. 51 Joseph named his firstborn Manasseh and said, "It is because God has made me forget all my trouble and all my father's household." 52 The second son he named Ephraim and said, "It is because God has made me fruitful in the land of my suffering."

53 The seven years of abundance in Egypt came to an end, 54 and the seven years of famine began, just as Joseph had said. There was famine

in all the other lands, but in the whole land of Egypt there was food. *55* When all Egypt began to feel the famine, the people cried to Pharaoh for food. Then Pharaoh told all the Egyptians, "Go to Joseph and do what he tells you."

*56* When the famine had spread over the whole country, Joseph opened all the storehouses and sold grain to the Egyptians, for the famine was severe throughout Egypt. *57* And all the world came to Egypt to buy grain from Joseph, because the famine was severe everywhere.

## Genesis 47:13–26

*13* There was no food, however, in the whole region because the famine was severe; both Egypt and Canaan wasted away because of the famine. *14* Joseph collected all the money that was to be found in Egypt and Canaan in payment for the grain they were buying, and he brought it to Pharaoh's palace. *15* When the money of the people of Egypt and Canaan was gone, all Egypt came to Joseph and said, "Give us food. Why should we die before your eyes? Our money is all gone."

*16* "Then bring your livestock," said Joseph. "I will sell you food in exchange for your livestock, since your money is gone." *17* So they brought their livestock to Joseph, and he gave them food in exchange for their horses, their sheep and goats, their cattle and donkeys. And he brought them through that year with food in exchange for all their livestock.

*18* When that year was over, they came to him the following year and said, "We cannot hide from our lord the fact that since our money is gone and our livestock belongs to you, there is nothing left for our lord except our bodies and our land. *19* Why should we perish before your eyes—we and our land as well? Buy us and our land in exchange for food, and we with our land will be in bondage to Pharaoh. Give us seed so that we may live and not die, and that the land may not become desolate."

*20* So Joseph bought all the land in Egypt for Pharaoh. The Egyptians, one and all, sold their fields, because the famine was too severe for them. The land became Pharaoh's, *21* and Joseph reduced the people to servitude, from one end of Egypt to the other. *22* However, he did not buy the land of the priests, *because they received a regular allotment from Pharaoh and had food enough from the allotment Pharaoh gave them. That is why they did not sell their land.*

*²³ Joseph said to the people, "Now that I have bought you and your land today for Pharaoh, here is seed for you so you can plant the ground. ²⁴ But when the crop comes in, give a fifth of it to Pharaoh. The other four-fifths you may keep as seed for the fields and as food for yourselves and your households and your children."*

*²⁵ "You have saved our lives," they said. "May we find favor in the eyes of our lord; we will be in bondage to Pharaoh."*

*²⁶ So Joseph established it as a law concerning land in Egypt—still in force today—that a fifth of the produce belongs to Pharaoh. It was only the land of the priests that did not become Pharaoh's.*

## Study Questions

1. Since Joseph gave God credit for the interpretation of Pharaoh's dream, does he still deserve to be recognized for having discernment? Explain your answer.

_____

_____

_____

_____

_____

_____

_____

2. In what way did Pharaoh exhibit discernment?

_____

_____

_____

_____

_____

_____

_____

3. Why do you think Joseph used the famine to acquire money, livestock, land, and even the people themselves for Pharaoh?

_____

_____

_____

_____

_____

4. Do you consider the terms Joseph established as Egypt's leader to be fair or exploitative? Explain your answer.

_____

_____

_____

_____

_____

_____

## ② Hiram and Solomon Strike a Deal

### 1 Kings 5:1–12

_1 When Hiram king of Tyre heard that Solomon had been anointed king to succeed his father David, he sent his envoys to Solomon, because he had always been on friendly terms with David. 2 Solomon sent back this message to Hiram:_

_3 "You know that because of the wars waged against my father David from all sides, he could not build a temple for the Name of the LORD his God until the LORD put his enemies under his feet. 4 But now the LORD my God has given me rest on every side, and there is no adversary or disaster. 5 I intend, therefore, to build a temple for the Name of the LORD my God, as the LORD told my father David, when he said, 'Your son whom I will put on the throne in your place will build the temple for my Name.'_

*⁶ "So give orders that cedars of Lebanon be cut for me. My men will work with yours, and I will pay you for your men whatever wages you set. You know that we have no one so skilled in felling timber as the Sidonians."*

*⁷ When Hiram heard Solomon's message, he was greatly pleased and said, "Praise be to the LORD today, for he has given David a wise son to rule over this great nation."*

*⁸ So Hiram sent word to Solomon:*

*"I have received the message you sent me and will do all you want in providing the cedar and juniper logs. ⁹ My men will haul them down from Lebanon to the Mediterranean Sea, and I will float them as rafts by sea to the place you specify. There I will separate them and you can take them away. And you are to grant my wish by providing food for my royal household."*

*¹⁰ In this way Hiram kept Solomon supplied with all the cedar and juniper logs he wanted, ¹¹ and Solomon gave Hiram twenty thousand cors of wheat as food for his household, in addition to twenty thousand baths of pressed olive oil. Solomon continued to do this for Hiram year after year. ¹² The LORD gave Solomon wisdom, just as he had promised him. There were peaceful relations between Hiram and Solomon, and the two of them made a treaty.*

## Study Questions

1. Why do you think Hiram initiated contact with Solomon by sending his envoys to the new king?

   _____

   _____

   _____

   _____

2. Who displayed greater discernment in this interaction: Hiram or Solomon? Why?

   _____

   _____

   _____

   _____

3. Do you think the deal they struck was even? Or did one of them do better than the other? Explain your answer.

_____

_____

_____

_____

## ③ Seek Wisdom and You Will Find It

### Proverbs 2:1–15

[1] *My son, if you accept my words*
   *and store up my commands within you,*
[2] *turning your ear to wisdom*
   *and applying your heart to understanding—*
[3] *indeed, if you call out for insight*
   *and cry aloud for understanding,*
[4] *and if you look for it as for silver*
   *and search for it as for hidden treasure,*
[5] *then you will understand the fear of the Lord*
   *and find the knowledge of God.*
[6] *For the Lord gives wisdom;*
   *from his mouth come knowledge and understanding.*
[7] *He holds success in store for the upright,*
   *he is a shield to those whose walk is blameless,*
[8] *for he guards the course of the just*
   *and protects the way of his faithful ones.*
[9] *Then you will understand what is right and just*
   *and fair—every good path.*
[10] *For wisdom will enter your heart,*
   *and knowledge will be pleasant to your soul.*
[11] *Discretion will protect you,*
   *and understanding will guard you.*

¹² *Wisdom will save you from the ways of wicked men,*
   *from men whose words are perverse,*
¹³ *who have left the straight paths*
   *to walk in dark ways,*
¹⁴ *who delight in doing wrong*
   *and rejoice in the perverseness of evil,*
¹⁵ *whose paths are crooked*
   *and who are devious in their ways.*

## Study Questions

1. Are there differences between *understanding*, *wisdom*, and *discernment*?
   If so, what are they?

   _____

   _____

   _____

   _____

2. According to this passage, how does a person grow in these qualities?

   _____

   _____

   _____

   _____

   _____

   _____

3. What are the rewards of these qualities?

   _____

   _____

   _____

   _____

   _____

4. Do you think it is possible for a leader to possess discernment and to have evil intentions at the same time? Explain.

_____

_____

_____

_____

_____

_____

# LEADERSHIP INSIGHT AND REFLECTION

How much of discernment is a gift from God, and how much can be acquired through experience, observation, and intentional growth?

_____

_____

_____

_____

_____

_____

_____

_____

_____

What role does prayer play in a leader's ability to use discernment?

_____

_____

_____

_____

_____

How discerning do you consider yourself to be on a scale of 1 (low) to 10 (high)? What is the basis of your self-evaluation?

_____

_____

_____

_____

_____

# TAKING ACTION

What are you currently neglecting to do that would make you become a more discerning leader? (Keep in mind James 1:5 says, "If any of you lacks wisdom, you should ask God, who gives generously to all without finding fault, and it will be given to you." At the very least, you should ask God to increase your wisdom.)

_____

_____

_____

_____

_____

What will you begin doing to increase your discernment?

_____

_____

_____

_____

_____

_____

_____

_____

_____

# GROUP DISCUSSION QUESTIONS

1. Most scholars believe Joseph had been a slave for more than a decade by the time Pharaoh summoned him to interpret his dream. If you had been Joseph, would you have been as open, forthcoming, and helpful as he was? Explain.

2. Why do you think Pharaoh appointed Joseph as his second-in-command instead of leading Egypt himself or choosing an Egyptian?

3. What words would you use to describe the interaction between Hiram and Solomon? Why did they treat each other the way they did?

4. The passage you read from Proverbs 2:1–15 suggests people should treat wisdom, understanding, and insight like treasure. How important have those qualities been to you up to now?

5. Where has lack of discernment let you down in the past? In particular, how has it hindered your leadership?

6. What have you done in the past to increase your discernment? What can you do now and in the future?

7. What specific action do you believe God is asking you to take to grow in discernment so that you can become a better leader? When and how will you do it?

# LESSON 8

# FOCUS

## The Sharper It Is, the Sharper You Are

## THE QUALITY DEFINED

Many people in leadership positions end up majoring in minor things, while others seem to major in nothing at all. Either they fixate on the wrong goals, or they don't seem to give any goal their full attention. Neither of these choices makes sense. To be effective, leaders need to develop focus, which is achieved when they are certain about their priorities and have a clear idea of how to pursue them. That kind of focus is targeted on two types of priorities: big-picture, long-term goals like vision and daily priorities such as important tasks on their to-do list.

For the long-term, effective leaders focus on what has the greatest impact. This usually means they devote more of their time, energy, and resources to growing in their strengths rather than in their areas of weakness. Obviously, every leader needs to give some attention to getting better at tasks that they're not good at. But that should not be their primary focus. Leaders often benefit most from delegating tasks in their areas of weakness rather than trying to master them.

As for the day-to-day, effective leaders resist the tyranny of the urgent. Because leadership is so complex and filled with urgent decisions, it's easy to be pulled off course by wrong priorities. So the first task is to determine what is really important—which is not necessarily the same as what is most urgent.

To maintain right priorities, determine your focus based on three questions. First, what is required of you? In other words, what part of your job can be done by you and you alone? Those tasks have high priority. Second, what gives you the greatest return on investment? What delivers a positive outcome that matches or exceeds the time and energy you give? After requirements, these tasks should come next. Finally, what gives you the greatest reward? What achievements would give you the greatest personal satisfaction? These are probably the tasks that you most want to do. If they are also requirements or high-return tasks, you're really on track.

Activity is not necessarily accomplishment. Effective leaders work hard to narrow their focus and give their attention to what really matters and has the most long-term impact.

# CASE STUDIES

Read these case studies from the Bible and answer the study questions that follow.

## ① Nehemiah Ignores the Opposition

### Nehemiah 6:1–15

[1] *When word came to Sanballat, Tobiah, Geshem the Arab and the rest of our enemies that I had rebuilt the wall and not a gap was left in it—though up to that time I had not set the doors in the gates—* [2] *Sanballat and Geshem sent me this message: "Come, let us meet together in one of the villages on the plain of Ono."*

*But they were scheming to harm me;* [3] *so I sent messengers to them with this reply: "I am carrying on a great project and cannot go down. Why should the work stop while I leave it and go down to you?"* [4] *Four times they sent me the same message, and each time I gave them the same answer.*

[5] *Then, the fifth time, Sanballat sent his aide to me with the same message, and in his hand was an unsealed letter* [6] *in which was written:*

*"It is reported among the nations—and Geshem says it is true—that you and the Jews are plotting to revolt, and therefore you are building the wall. Moreover, according to these reports you are about to become*

*their king* [7] *and have even appointed prophets to make this proclamation about you in Jerusalem: 'There is a king in Judah!' Now this report will get back to the king; so come, let us meet together."*

[8] *I sent him this reply: "Nothing like what you are saying is happening; you are just making it up out of your head."*

[9] *They were all trying to frighten us, thinking, "Their hands will get too weak for the work, and it will not be completed."*

*But I prayed, "Now strengthen my hands."*

[10] *One day I went to the house of Shemaiah son of Delaiah, the son of Mehetabel, who was shut in at his home. He said, "Let us meet in the house of God, inside the temple, and let us close the temple doors, because men are coming to kill you—by night they are coming to kill you."*

[11] *But I said, "Should a man like me run away? Or should someone like me go into the temple to save his life? I will not go!"* [12] *I realized that God had not sent him, but that he had prophesied against me because Tobiah and Sanballat had hired him.* [13] *He had been hired to intimidate me so that I would commit a sin by doing this, and then they would give me a bad name to discredit me.*

[14] *Remember Tobiah and Sanballat, my God, because of what they have done; remember also the prophet Noadiah and how she and the rest of the prophets have been trying to intimidate me.* [15] *So the wall was completed on the twenty-fifth of Elul, in fifty-two days.*

## Study Questions

1. How many different ways in this passage did Nehemiah's opponents try to stop him from his work rebuilding the walls and gates of Jerusalem? What were they?

2. What was Nehemiah's thinking in response to each attempt?

_____

_____

_____

_____

_____

3. What do you think motivated Nehemiah's opponents?

_____

_____

_____

_____

4. What motivated and enabled Nehemiah to remain focused in response to opposition?

_____

_____

_____

_____

## 2 Jesus Helps Peter Regain His Focus

### John 21:1–22

[1] Afterward Jesus appeared again to his disciples, by the Sea of Galilee. It happened this way: [2] Simon Peter, Thomas (also known as Didymus), Nathanael from Cana in Galilee, the sons of Zebedee, and two other disciples were together. [3] "I'm going out to fish," Simon Peter told them, and they said, "We'll go with you." So they went out and got into the boat, but that night they caught nothing.

[4] Early in the morning, Jesus stood on the shore, but the disciples did not realize that it was Jesus.

⁵ He called out to them, "Friends, haven't you any fish?"

"No," they answered.

⁶ He said, "Throw your net on the right side of the boat and you will find some." When they did, they were unable to haul the net in because of the large number of fish.

⁷ Then the disciple whom Jesus loved said to Peter, "It is the Lord!" As soon as Simon Peter heard him say, "It is the Lord," he wrapped his outer garment around him (for he had taken it off) and jumped into the water. ⁸ The other disciples followed in the boat, towing the net full of fish, for they were not far from shore, about a hundred yards. ⁹ When they landed, they saw a fire of burning coals there with fish on it, and some bread.

¹⁰ Jesus said to them, "Bring some of the fish you have just caught." ¹¹ So Simon Peter climbed back into the boat and dragged the net ashore. It was full of large fish, 153, but even with so many the net was not torn. ¹² Jesus said to them, "Come and have breakfast." None of the disciples dared ask him, "Who are you?" They knew it was the Lord. ¹³ Jesus came, took the bread and gave it to them, and did the same with the fish. ¹⁴ This was now the third time Jesus appeared to his disciples after he was raised from the dead.

¹⁵ When they had finished eating, Jesus said to Simon Peter, "Simon son of John, do you love me more than these?"

"Yes, Lord," he said, "you know that I love you."

Jesus said, "Feed my lambs."

¹⁶ Again Jesus said, "Simon son of John, do you love me?"

He answered, "Yes, Lord, you know that I love you."

Jesus said, "Take care of my sheep."

¹⁷ The third time he said to him, "Simon son of John, do you love me?"

Peter was hurt because Jesus asked him the third time, "Do you love me?" He said, "Lord, you know all things; you know that I love you."

Jesus said, "Feed my sheep. ¹⁸ Very truly I tell you, when you were younger you dressed yourself and went where you wanted; but when you are old you will stretch out your hands, and someone else will dress you and lead you where you do not want to go." ¹⁹ Jesus said this to indicate the kind of death by which Peter would glorify God. Then he said to him, "Follow me!"

²⁰ Peter turned and saw that the disciple whom Jesus loved was following them. (This was the one who had leaned back against Jesus at the supper and

had said, "Lord, who is going to betray you?") ²¹ When Peter saw him, he asked, "Lord, what about him?"

²² Jesus answered, "If I want him to remain alive until I return, what is that to you? You must follow me."

## Study Questions

1. Do you think Peter had gone back to fishing as a full-time endeavor, or did he and his companions just happen to be fishing when Jesus visited them? Explain.

2. Why do you think Jesus chose to fill their net to overflowing with fish?

3. How much of a problem do you think staying focused was for Peter? What evidence do you find in this passage to support your opinion? What other things have you read about him to support your opinion?

4. Why did Jesus ask Peter the question three times? Was it effective?

_____

_____

_____

# ③ Paul Puts His Life in Perspective

## Philippians 3:7–14

*⁷ But whatever were gains to me I now consider loss for the sake of Christ. ⁸ What is more, I consider everything a loss because of the surpassing worth of knowing Christ Jesus my Lord, for whose sake I have lost all things. I consider them garbage, that I may gain Christ ⁹ and be found in him, not having a righteousness of my own that comes from the law, but that which is through faith in Christ—the righteousness that comes from God on the basis of faith. ¹⁰ I want to know Christ—yes, to know the power of his resurrection and participation in his sufferings, becoming like him in his death, ¹¹ and so, somehow, attaining to the resurrection from the dead.*

*¹² Not that I have already obtained all this, or have already arrived at my goal, but I press on to take hold of that for which Christ Jesus took hold of me. ¹³ Brothers and sisters, I do not consider myself yet to have taken hold of it. But one thing I do: Forgetting what is behind and straining toward what is ahead, ¹⁴ I press on toward the goal to win the prize for which God has called me heavenward in Christ Jesus.*

## Study Questions

1. What does Paul mean when he says that the things that he considered gains are now loss to him?

_____

_____

_____

_____

_____

2. How does his statement relate to focus? How does it relate to priorities?
How are those two things different?

_____

_____

_____

_____

_____

_____

_____

3. What does Paul say he is focusing on? Why?

_____

_____

_____

_____

_____

4. How do you think Paul's focus relates to his leadership?

_____

_____

_____

_____

# LEADERSHIP INSIGHT AND REFLECTION

Do you identify with any of the leaders in the passages? If so, which one, and why?

_____

_____

_____

How were the three leaders in these passages able to remain focused? You may want to credit their ability to God's call on their lives, but that doesn't explain everything. Every person who believes in God and chooses to follow him can be said to have a call of God on his or her life, yet many don't remain focused on fulfilling it. What empowered these leaders to be effective?

_____

_____

_____

_____

# Taking Action

In what area of your life or leadership is God asking you to improve your focus?

_____

_____

_____

How would improvement in this area benefit you and others?

_____

_____

_____

_____

What concrete immediate step will you take to improve? When will you take it?

_____

_____

_____

_____

# Group Discussion Questions

1. Nehemiah's response to Sanballat, Tobiah, and Geshem the Arab appears to be very dismissive. How much do you think their comments actually bothered Nehemiah?

2. What might have happened if Nehemiah had been distracted by his enemies? Would the walls, which had lain in ruins for more than a century, still have been rebuilt in fifty-two days? Why or why not?

3. Why do you think Jesus addressed his questions only to Peter when other disciples were there with him fishing?

4. Paul accomplished a lot in his lifetime. Why would he call "everything a loss" and "garbage" (Philippians 3:8)? How does Paul's thinking impact yours?

5. For each of these leaders, were the catalysts that helped them to focus something internal, external, or both? Explain.

6. What catalysts do you seek or practices do you follow to help you to focus? In which areas of your life are they successful? In which areas aren't they successful?

7. How do you need to change to become better at focusing on accomplishing what God desires you to do? What will you do and when will you do it?

# LESSON 9

# GENEROSITY

### Your Candle Loses Nothing
### When It Lights Another

## THE QUALITY DEFINED

Nothing speaks to followers more loudly or serves them better than generosity from their leader. True generosity communicates that the leader cares about people's well-being and has unselfish motives. This builds both loyalty and high morale. And followers tend to respond with a willingness to give back to the leader. People don't care how much you know until they know how much you care. Generosity is a concrete demonstration of how much the leader cares.

Some people are more naturally generous than others. But anyone can develop greater generosity. The first step is a change in perspective. Generous leaders are content. They are not preoccupied with obtaining or hoarding wealth. Instead, they are happy and grateful for what they have. They see money as a gift, and as a result they hold on to it loosely.

Generous leaders always value their people more than their possessions. They put their followers first. They also see money for what it is: a resource or tool. They understand that its value comes from its ability to advance a greater mission. As a result, they are not mastered by money, but rather use it to serve their people and the vision.

The best way to become more generous is to become consistent in the practice of generosity. Make it a habit. The amount given is not as important as the act of giving. Find ways to be generous every day, and you will benefit both as a leader and as a person. And don't limit your generosity to money. Offer your time, knowledge, and resources as well. Writer John Bunyan said, "You have not lived today until you have done something for someone who can never repay you." Live at a higher level by being generous. Giving is truly the highest level of living.

# CASE STUDIES

Read these case studies from the Bible and answer the study questions that follow.

## 1 Boaz Gives Willingly

### Ruth 2:1–18

*1 Now Naomi had a relative on her husband's side, a man of standing from the clan of Elimelek, whose name was Boaz.*

*2 And Ruth the Moabite said to Naomi, "Let me go to the fields and pick up the leftover grain behind anyone in whose eyes I find favor."*

*Naomi said to her, "Go ahead, my daughter." 3 So she went out, entered a field and began to glean behind the harvesters. As it turned out, she was working in a field belonging to Boaz, who was from the clan of Elimelek.*

*4 Just then Boaz arrived from Bethlehem and greeted the harvesters, "The LORD be with you!"*

*"The LORD bless you!" they answered.*

*5 Boaz asked the overseer of his harvesters, "Who does that young woman belong to?"*

*6 The overseer replied, "She is the Moabite who came back from Moab with Naomi. 7 She said, 'Please let me glean and gather among the sheaves behind the harvesters.' She came into the field and has remained here from morning till now, except for a short rest in the shelter."*

*8 So Boaz said to Ruth, "My daughter, listen to me. Don't go and glean in another field and don't go away from here. Stay here with the women who work for me. 9 Watch the field where the men are harvesting, and follow along after the women. I have told the men not to lay a hand on you. And whenever you are thirsty, go and get a drink from the water jars the men have filled."*

*10 At this, she bowed down with her face to the ground. She asked him, "Why have I found such favor in your eyes that you notice me—a foreigner?"*

*11 Boaz replied, "I've been told all about what you have done for your mother-in-law since the death of your husband—how you left your father and mother and your homeland and came to live with a people you did not know before. 12 May the LORD repay you for what you have done. May you be richly rewarded by the LORD, the God of Israel, under whose wings you have come to take refuge."*

*13 "May I continue to find favor in your eyes, my lord," she said. "You have put me at ease by speaking kindly to your servant—though I do not have the standing of one of your servants."*

*14 At mealtime Boaz said to her, "Come over here. Have some bread and dip it in the wine vinegar."*

*When she sat down with the harvesters, he offered her some roasted grain. She ate all she wanted and had some left over. 15 As she got up to glean, Boaz gave orders to his men, "Let her gather among the sheaves and don't reprimand her. 16 Even pull out some stalks for her from the bundles and leave them for her to pick up, and don't rebuke her."*

*17 So Ruth gleaned in the field until evening. Then she threshed the barley she had gathered, and it amounted to about an ephah. 18 She carried it back to town, and her mother-in-law saw how much she had gathered. Ruth also brought out and gave her what she had left over after she had eaten enough.*

## Study Questions

1. God had told his people, "When you reap the harvest of your land, do not reap to the very edges of your field or gather the gleanings of your harvest. Leave them for the poor and for the foreigner residing among you"

(Leviticus 23:22). In this passage, was Boaz simply obeying God, or was he being generous? Explain.

_____

_____

_____

2. Why do you think Boaz acted the way he did?

_____

_____

_____

_____

3. What do you think Boaz's laborers thought of his actions? Would their esteem of him have risen or fallen because of what he did? Why?

_____

_____

_____

_____

## ❷ The Heart of Giving

### Acts 4:32–37

*³² All the believers were one in heart and mind. No one claimed that any of their possessions was their own, but they shared everything they had. ³³ With great power the apostles continued to testify to the resurrection of the Lord Jesus. And God's grace was so powerfully at work in them all ³⁴ that there were no needy persons among them. For from time to time those who owned land or houses sold them, brought the money from the sales ³⁵ and put it at the apostles' feet, and it was distributed to anyone who had need.*

*[36]* *Joseph, a Levite from Cyprus, whom the apostles called Barnabas (which means "son of encouragement"), [37] sold a field he owned and brought the money and put it at the apostles' feet.*

## Acts 5:1–11

*[1] Now a man named Ananias, together with his wife Sapphira, also sold a piece of property. [2] With his wife's full knowledge he kept back part of the money for himself, but brought the rest and put it at the apostles' feet.*

*[3] Then Peter said, "Ananias, how is it that Satan has so filled your heart that you have lied to the Holy Spirit and have kept for yourself some of the money you received for the land? [4] Didn't it belong to you before it was sold? And after it was sold, wasn't the money at your disposal? What made you think of doing such a thing? You have not lied just to human beings but to God."*

*[5] When Ananias heard this, he fell down and died. And great fear seized all who heard what had happened. [6] Then some young men came forward, wrapped up his body, and carried him out and buried him.*

*[7] About three hours later his wife came in, not knowing what had happened. [8] Peter asked her, "Tell me, is this the price you and Ananias got for the land?"*

*"Yes," she said, "that is the price."*

*[9] Peter said to her, "How could you conspire to test the Spirit of the Lord? Listen! The feet of the men who buried your husband are at the door, and they will carry you out also."*

*[10] At that moment she fell down at his feet and died. Then the young men came in and, finding her dead, carried her out and buried her beside her husband. [11] Great fear seized the whole church and all who heard about these events.*

## Study Questions

1. What do you think motivated Joseph, also called Barnabas, when he sold his field and brought the proceeds from the sale to the apostles?

   _____

   _____

   _____

2. Why did Peter confront Ananias when he brought money to the apostles after selling his land? What was the difference between his action and Joseph's? Why wasn't Ananias' action generous and acceptable?

_____

_____

_____

_____

3. What was Ananias' sin? What was Sapphira's? What could Ananias and Sapphira have done differently to avoid the fate they suffered?

_____

_____

_____

_____

_____

4. Why do you think Ananias and Sapphira were punished so harshly? Do you think Peter *asked* God to strike them down? Or do you think he simply *knew* God intended to punish them in this way?

_____

_____

_____

_____

## ③ Paul Encourages Generosity

### 2 Corinthians 8:1–15

---

[1] *And now, brothers and sisters, we want you to know about the grace that God has given the Macedonian churches.* [2] *In the midst of a very severe trial, their*

*overflowing joy and their extreme poverty welled up in rich generosity. ³ For I testify that they gave as much as they were able, and even beyond their ability. Entirely on their own, ⁴ they urgently pleaded with us for the privilege of sharing in this service to the Lord's people. ⁵ And they exceeded our expectations: They gave themselves first of all to the Lord, and then by the will of God also to us. ⁶ So we urged Titus, just as he had earlier made a beginning, to bring also to completion this act of grace on your part. ⁷ But since you excel in everything— in faith, in speech, in knowledge, in complete earnestness and in the love we have kindled in you—see that you also excel in this grace of giving.*

*⁸ I am not commanding you, but I want to test the sincerity of your love by comparing it with the earnestness of others. ⁹ For you know the grace of our Lord Jesus Christ, that though he was rich, yet for your sake he became poor, so that you through his poverty might become rich.*

*¹⁰ And here is my judgment about what is best for you in this matter. Last year you were the first not only to give but also to have the desire to do so. ¹¹ Now finish the work, so that your eager willingness to do it may be matched by your completion of it, according to your means. ¹² For if the willingness is there, the gift is acceptable according to what one has, not according to what one does not have.*

*¹³ Our desire is not that others might be relieved while you are hard pressed, but that there might be equality. ¹⁴ At the present time your plenty will supply what they need, so that in turn their plenty will supply what you need. The goal is equality, ¹⁵ as it is written: "The one who gathered much did not have too much, and the one who gathered little did not have too little."*

## Study Questions

1. What is the role of wealth in generosity? What is the role of attitude? Which is more important?

   _____

   _____

   _____

   _____

   _____

   _____

   _____

2. Why do you think Paul admonishes the Corinthians to finish the work of giving?

_____

_____

_____

_____

3. What part does giving oneself first to God play when it comes to being generous to others?

_____

_____

_____

_____

# LEADERSHIP INSIGHT AND REFLECTION

What factors come into play when it comes to generosity? How important is financial status? How did it impact the giving of the leaders in these passages?

_____

_____

_____

_____

What role did attitude play?

_____

_____

_____

_____

_____

_____

What about opportunity or need? Are there other factors that come into play? If so, what are they?

_____

_____

_____

_____

_____

What is one statement you could write that summarizes a biblical philosophy of generosity?

_____

_____

_____

_____

# TAKING ACTION

Where are you not practicing generosity the way you could or should be? How are you falling short as a person? How could you be more generous as a leader?

_____

_____

_____

_____

_____

What can you do as a *daily practice* for the next thirty days to become more generous?

_____

_____

_____

_____

_____

_____

# GROUP DISCUSSION QUESTIONS

1. In what ways did Boaz fulfill the law stated in Leviticus 23:22? In what ways did he exceed it?

2. How would you characterize Ruth's response to Boaz? Do you think Boaz's actions might have changed if her response to him had been different? If you were in his shoes, would yours have changed?

3. Do you think the punishment of Ananias and Sapphira fit their crime? Explain.

4. Why do you think Paul wrote to the Corinthians about giving and generosity? Why did he include what he said about Jesus?

5. How do you think generosity or its lack impacts a leader's ability to be effective? Explain.

6. What was your greatest takeaway about generosity you gained from this lesson?

7. What action will you take to become more generous? When and how will you do it?

# LESSON 10

# INITIATIVE

## You Won't Leave Home without It

### THE QUALITY DEFINED

Leaders initiate. Someone has to go first, and the one who does is usually seen as the leader. To take initiative is to go beyond noticing a problem or seeing a need. Successful leaders take action on what they see—often before anyone else does. This comes more easily for some personalities. But even people more prone to contemplation can learn to take action.

Effective leaders are always on the lookout for opportunities. They know what they want, and they see everything through the filter of opportunity. Even in the midst of hardship or failure, they ask themselves, "How can I use this situation to move forward toward the goal?" And once they see an opportunity, they immediately look for ways to seize it. They are decisive, and they refuse to give in to the "paralysis of analysis." After deciding to act, they don't wait for anyone else to motivate them. They push themselves to take action, even if it takes them beyond their comfort zone.

To succeed at taking initiative, leaders must face the fear of failure and overcome it. They understand that mistakes are possible, and they weigh the risk accurately. Then they take action accordingly. One reason for this is that they recognize the price of not acting. Usually, it is higher than imperfect action. And not making a decision often leads to the decision being made by others for them.

The good news for initiators is that they make things happen. The bad news is that they make lots of mistakes. IBM founder Thomas J. Watson said, "The way to succeed is to double your failure rate." The greater the potential for success, the greater the chance for failure. As Senator Robert Kennedy said, "Only those who dare to fail greatly can ever achieve greatly." If you want to achieve great things as a leader, you've got to be willing to initiate and put yourself on the line.

# CASE STUDIES

Read these case studies from the Bible and answer the study questions that follow.

## ① Noah's Bold Actions

### Genesis 6:9–22

*9 This is the account of Noah and his family.*

*Noah was a righteous man, blameless among the people of his time, and he walked faithfully with God. 10 Noah had three sons: Shem, Ham and Japheth.*

*11 Now the earth was corrupt in God's sight and was full of violence. 12 God saw how corrupt the earth had become, for all the people on earth had corrupted their ways. 13 So God said to Noah, "I am going to put an end to all people, for the earth is filled with violence because of them. I am surely going to destroy both them and the earth. 14 So make yourself an ark of cypress wood; make rooms in it and coat it with pitch inside and out. 15 This is how you are to build it: The ark is to be three hundred cubits long, fifty cubits wide and thirty cubits high. 16 Make a roof for it, leaving below the roof an opening one cubit high all around. Put a door in the side of the ark and make lower, middle and upper decks. 17 I am going to bring floodwaters on the earth to destroy all life under the heavens, every creature that has the breath of life in it. Everything on earth will perish. 18 But I will establish my covenant with you, and you will enter the ark—you and your sons and your wife and your sons' wives with you. 19 You are to bring into the ark two of all living creatures, male and female, to keep them alive with you.* ²⁰ *Two of every kind of bird, of every kind of animal and of every kind of creature that moves along the ground will come to you to be kept alive.* ²¹ *You are to take every kind of food that is to be eaten and store it away as food for you and for them."*

²² *Noah did everything just as God commanded him.*

## Genesis 7:1–5

¹ *The LORD then said to Noah, "Go into the ark, you and your whole family, because I have found you righteous in this generation.* ² *Take with you seven pairs of every kind of clean animal, a male and its mate, and one pair of every kind of unclean animal, a male and its mate,* ³ *and also seven pairs of every kind of bird, male and female, to keep their various kinds alive throughout the earth.* ⁴ *Seven days from now I will send rain on the earth for forty days and forty nights, and I will wipe from the face of the earth every living creature I have made."*

⁵ *And Noah did all that the LORD commanded him.*

## Study Questions

1. How do you think Noah felt as God described the coming flood and gave directions for what was to be done to prepare for it?

   _____

   _____

   _____

   _____

   _____

   _____

   _____

   _____

   _____

   _____

2. The passage simply states, "Noah did everything just as God commanded him" (6:22; see also 7:5). Fill in the gaps by listing the ways in which you

imagine Noah had to act with initiative in order to fulfill God's instructions. What would he have had to figure out and do as a leader?

_____

_____

_____

_____

3. How do you think the conversation went with Noah's wife, his three sons, and their wives when he initiated the ark project? When it was time to gather the animals? When he wanted them to get into the ark before it started to rain?

_____

_____

_____

_____

_____

_____

4. What leadership abilities did Noah need to complete this task? List them.

_____

_____

_____

_____

_____

_____

_____

_____

## 2 Isaiah Steps Forward

### Isaiah 6:1–13

*¹ In the year that King Uzziah died, I saw the Lord, high and exalted, seated on a throne; and the train of his robe filled the temple. ² Above him were seraphim, each with six wings: With two wings they covered their faces, with two they covered their feet, and with two they were flying. ³ And they were calling to one another:*

> *"Holy, holy, holy is the LORD Almighty;*
> *the whole earth is full of his glory."*

*⁴ At the sound of their voices the doorposts and thresholds shook and the temple was filled with smoke.*

*⁵ "Woe to me!" I cried. "I am ruined! For I am a man of unclean lips, and I live among a people of unclean lips, and my eyes have seen the King, the LORD Almighty."*

*⁶ Then one of the seraphim flew to me with a live coal in his hand, which he had taken with tongs from the altar. ⁷ With it he touched my mouth and said, "See, this has touched your lips; your guilt is taken away and your sin atoned for."*

*⁸ Then I heard the voice of the Lord saying, "Whom shall I send? And who will go for us?"*

*And I said, "Here am I. Send me!"*

*⁹ He said, "Go and tell this people:*

> *" 'Be ever hearing, but never understanding;*
> *be ever seeing, but never perceiving.'*
> *¹⁰ Make the heart of this people calloused;*
> *make their ears dull*
> *and close their eyes.*
> *Otherwise they might see with their eyes,*
> *hear with their ears,*
> *understand with their hearts,*
> *and turn and be healed."*

*[11] Then I said, "For how long, Lord?"*
*And he answered:*

*"Until the cities lie ruined*
*and without inhabitant,*
*until the houses are left deserted*
*and the fields ruined and ravaged,*
*[12] until the LORD has sent everyone far away*
*and the land is utterly forsaken.*
*[13] And though a tenth remains in the land,*
*it will again be laid waste.*
*But as the terebinth and oak*
*leave stumps when they are cut down,*
*so the holy seed will be the stump in the land."*

## Study Questions

1. Isaiah was terrified by what he saw, yet he volunteered when the Lord
   looked for someone to send as his representative. Why?

   _____

   _____

   _____

   _____

   _____

2. The task the Lord gave to Isaiah was not a pleasant one; the message was
   not happy and uplifting. How do you think Isaiah felt when he understood
   what he was to do?

   _____

   _____

   _____

   _____

   _____

   _____

3. We know from the rest of the book that bears his name that Isaiah the prophet fulfilled the mission the Lord gave him. What do you think sustained him?

_____

_____

_____

_____

_____

_____

## 3 James Extols the Value of Taking Action

### James 2:14–26

[14] What good is it, my brothers and sisters, if someone claims to have faith but has no deeds? Can such faith save them? [15] Suppose a brother or a sister is without clothes and daily food. [16] If one of you says to them, "Go in peace; keep warm and well fed," but does nothing about their physical needs, what good is it? [17] In the same way, faith by itself, if it is not accompanied by action, is dead.

[18] But someone will say, "You have faith; I have deeds."

Show me your faith without deeds, and I will show you my faith by my deeds. [19] You believe that there is one God. Good! Even the demons believe that—and shudder.

[20] You foolish person, do you want evidence that faith without deeds is useless? [21] Was not our father Abraham considered righteous for what he did when he offered his son Isaac on the altar? [22] You see that his faith and his actions were working together, and his faith was made complete by what he did. [23] And the scripture was fulfilled that says, "Abraham believed God, and it was credited to him as righteousness," and he was called God's friend. [24] You see that a person is considered righteous by what they do and not by faith alone.

[25] In the same way, was not even Rahab the prostitute considered righteous for what she did when she gave lodging to the spies and sent them off in a different direction? [26] As the body without the spirit is dead, so faith without deeds is dead.

## Study Questions

1. James calls faith without deeds worthless and dead (see verse 17). What is your gut reaction to his assertions?

_____

_____

_____

_____

_____

_____

_____

2. Believers cannot take action on every need they see or idea they have. How should they decide when to initiate?

_____

_____

_____

_____

_____

_____

_____

3. What is the application of James' ideas to leadership? How should a leader decide when to translate an idea into action through initiative?

_____

_____

_____

_____

_____

_____

_____

_____

# LEADERSHIP INSIGHT AND REFLECTION

Think about the role of vision when it comes to showing initiative. In each of the passages, the leaders had different experiences with vision. Noah received a direct message from God. Isaiah experienced a literal vision and reacted to it. James wrote about seeing a practical need and responding to it. How does vision typically come to you? And how do you process it?

_____

_____

_____

_____

_____

_____

_____

_____

_____

_____

_____

How important was courage in the leaders for them to initiate action in the passages you read? How much of a factor is it for you when you need to act?

_____

_____

_____

_____

_____

_____

_____

_____

_____

_____

The leaders in the passages not only initiated, but they also *sustained* action. How difficult do you think that was for them? How difficult is it for you?

_____

_____

_____

_____

_____

_____

_____

_____

_____

_____

_____

# TAKING ACTION

Where do you most need to grow as a leader to become better at showing initiative? Do you need greater vision? Do you need greater courage? Do you need more confidence or energy so that you can finish what you start? Describe where you need to grow.

_____

_____

_____

_____

_____

_____

_____

_____

_____

_____

_____

_____

_____

What action will you take immediately to grow in that area?

_____

_____

_____

_____

_____

_____

_____

_____

_____

_____

_____

_____

_____

_____

# GROUP DISCUSSION QUESTIONS

1. What do you think Noah's attitude and mindset were as he worked on the ark?

2. Jesus said that in Noah's time, people were eating, drinking, marrying and being given in marriage up to the day Noah entered the ark (see Luke 17:26–27). How do you think people reacted to what Noah was doing? If you were in Noah's place, how would people's reactions have impacted you?

3. What do you think would have happened if Isaiah had not stepped forward and said, "Here am I. Send me" (Isaiah 6:8)?

4. What was your emotional response to James's statement that if we see someone without clothes or food and only wish them well yet do nothing that it does no good?

5. In light of James's comments about deeds, how would you assess the status of your faith? Your leadership?

6. What was your greatest spiritual takeaway from this lesson? What was your greatest leadership takeaway?

7. What action do you believe God is asking you to take to improve your leadership in the area of initiative as a result of this lesson? When and how will you do it?

# LESSON 11

# LISTENING

## It's Sometimes Better to Receive than Give

## THE QUALITY DEFINED

Are you a good listener? I know when I started in leadership, I wasn't. I was too busy doing my own thing and trying to make things happen. Because my vision for where we could go was so strong, I tended to talk more than I listened. I had things I wanted to say. And I knew they would benefit my followers! But I soon learned that my unwillingness to listen was damaging my ability to connect with my followers. And because I didn't ask for or welcome input, I was also missing opportunities to learn from other people's wisdom.

Communication is a two-way street. It must include both talking and listening if people are going to connect. And connection is critical to effective leadership, because people will not willingly follow a leader who has not connected with them. As I've often said, leaders touch a heart before they ask for a hand. Before leaders can touch a person's heart, they have to know what's in it. When you make listening a priority, you understand people better. You know their desires and concerns. That makes it possible for you to meet those needs. In addition, intentional listening communicates to others that their feelings and input matter.

Besides connection, listening encourages learning. Wise leaders understand that they can always learn something from others. Two heads are better than one. And many minds are even better. When you listen to the words of others—from advice and requests to complaints and disagreement—you receive information you can use. Listening provides data that can help refine and improve a leader's vision and plans.

Who should you listen to? Obviously, good leaders listen to their followers. But they also listen to the people that their organization serves, especially when those people complain. Microsoft co-founder Bill Gates said, "Unhappy customers are always a concern. They're also your greatest opportunity." Effective leaders encourage others to tell them what they need to know, not just what they want to hear. They accept and value disagreement. Finally, effective leaders pay close attention to the words of their mentors. When those ahead of you share their advice and their failures, it's a gift that can help you to avoid their mistakes and learn from their successes.

# CASE STUDIES

Read these case studies from the Bible and answer the study questions that follow.

 ## Lessons in Listening

### 1 Samuel 3:1–21

> ¹ *The boy Samuel ministered before the Lord under Eli. In those days the word of the LORD was rare; there were not many visions.*
> ² *One night Eli, whose eyes were becoming so weak that he could barely see, was lying down in his usual place.* ³ *The lamp of God had not yet gone out, and Samuel was lying down in the house of the LORD, where the ark of God was.* ⁴ *Then the LORD called Samuel.*
> *Samuel answered, "Here I am."* ⁵ *And he ran to Eli and said, "Here I am; you called me."*
> *But Eli said, "I did not call; go back and lie down." So he went and lay down.*
> ⁶ *Again the LORD called, "Samuel!" And Samuel got up and went to Eli and said, "Here I am; you called me."*
> *"My son," Eli said, "I did not call; go back and lie down."*
> ⁷ *Now Samuel did not yet know the LORD: The word of the LORD had not yet been revealed to him.*

*⁸A third time the Lᴏʀᴅ called, "Samuel!" And Samuel got up and went to Eli and said, "Here I am; you called me."*

*Then Eli realized that the Lᴏʀᴅ was calling the boy. ⁹ So Eli told Samuel, "Go and lie down, and if he calls you, say, 'Speak, Lᴏʀᴅ, for your servant is listening.'" So Samuel went and lay down in his place.*

*¹⁰ The Lord came and stood there, calling as at the other times, "Samuel! Samuel!"*

*Then Samuel said, "Speak, for your servant is listening."*

*¹¹ And the Lᴏʀᴅ said to Samuel: "See, I am about to do something in Israel that will make the ears of everyone who hears about it tingle. ¹² At that time I will carry out against Eli everything I spoke against his family—from beginning to end. ¹³ For I told him that I would judge his family forever because of the sin he knew about; his sons blasphemed God, and he failed to restrain them. ¹⁴ Therefore I swore to the house of Eli, 'The guilt of Eli's house will never be atoned for by sacrifice or offering.'"*

*¹⁵ Samuel lay down until morning and then opened the doors of the house of the Lᴏʀᴅ. He was afraid to tell Eli the vision, ¹⁶ but Eli called him and said, "Samuel, my son."*

*Samuel answered, "Here I am."*

*¹⁷ "What was it he said to you?" Eli asked. "Do not hide it from me. May God deal with you, be it ever so severely, if you hide from me anything he told you." ¹⁸ So Samuel told him everything, hiding nothing from him. Then Eli said, "He is the Lᴏʀᴅ; let him do what is good in his eyes."*

*¹⁹ The Lᴏʀᴅ was with Samuel as he grew up, and he let none of Samuel's words fall to the ground. ²⁰ And all Israel from Dan to Beersheba recognized that Samuel was attested as a prophet of the Lᴏʀᴅ. ²¹ The Lᴏʀᴅ continued to appear at Shiloh, and there he revealed himself to Samuel through his word.*

## Study Questions

1. Why did it take so long for Samuel to understand that the Lord was speaking to him? Why did it take Eli so long?

   _____

   _____

   _____

2. What lessons about listening did Samuel learn in this passage? What lessons did Eli learn?

_____

_____

_____

_____

3. The passage indicates that God continued to speak to Samuel after he was a boy. Why do you think that happened? What made it possible?

_____

_____

_____

_____

4. The passage says that God "let none of Samuel's words fall to the ground" (verse 19), which means that what he said was always reliable. What effect do you think that had on people's willingness to listen to Samuel?

_____

_____

_____

_____

## ② Inconsistent Listener

### 2 Chronicles 25:1–2, 5–24, 27–28

¹ *Amaziah was twenty-five years old when he became king [of Judah], and he reigned in Jerusalem twenty-nine years. . . . ² He did what was right in the eyes of the Lord, but not wholeheartedly. . . .*

*5 Amaziah called the people of Judah together and assigned them according to their families to commanders of thousands and commanders of hundreds for all Judah and Benjamin. He then mustered those twenty years old or more and found that there were three hundred thousand men fit for military service, able to handle the spear and shield. 6 He also hired a hundred thousand fighting men from Israel for a hundred talents of silver.*

*7 But a man of God came to him and said, "Your Majesty, these troops from Israel must not march with you, for the Lord is not with Israel—not with any of the people of Ephraim. 8 Even if you go and fight courageously in battle, God will overthrow you before the enemy, for God has the power to help or to overthrow."*

*9 Amaziah asked the man of God, "But what about the hundred talents I paid for these Israelite troops?"*

*The man of God replied, "The Lord can give you much more than that."*

*10 So Amaziah dismissed the troops who had come to him from Ephraim and sent them home. They were furious with Judah and left for home in a great rage.*

*11 Amaziah then marshaled his strength and led his army to the Valley of Salt, where he killed ten thousand men of Seir. 12 The army of Judah also captured ten thousand men alive, took them to the top of a cliff and threw them down so that all were dashed to pieces.*

*13 Meanwhile the troops that Amaziah had sent back and had not allowed to take part in the war raided towns belonging to Judah from Samaria to Beth Horon. They killed three thousand people and carried off great quantities of plunder.*

*14 When Amaziah returned from slaughtering the Edomites, he brought back the gods of the people of Seir. He set them up as his own gods, bowed down to them and burned sacrifices to them. 15 The anger of the Lord burned against Amaziah, and he sent a prophet to him, who said, "Why do you consult this people's gods, which could not save their own people from your hand?"*

*16 While he was still speaking, the king said to him, "Have we appointed you an adviser to the king? Stop! Why be struck down?"*

*So the prophet stopped but said, "I know that God has determined to destroy you, because you have done this and have not listened to my counsel."*

*¹⁷ After Amaziah king of Judah consulted his advisers, he sent this challenge to Jehoash son of Jehoahaz, the son of Jehu, king of Israel: "Come, let us face each other in battle."*

*¹⁸ But Jehoash king of Israel replied to Amaziah king of Judah: "A thistle in Lebanon sent a message to a cedar in Lebanon, 'Give your daughter to my son in marriage.' Then a wild beast in Lebanon came along and trampled the thistle underfoot. ¹⁹ You say to yourself that you have defeated Edom, and now you are arrogant and proud. But stay at home! Why ask for trouble and cause your own downfall and that of Judah also?"*

*²⁰ Amaziah, however, would not listen, for God so worked that he might deliver them into the hands of Jehoash, because they sought the gods of Edom. ²¹ So Jehoash king of Israel attacked. He and Amaziah king of Judah faced each other at Beth Shemesh in Judah. ²² Judah was routed by Israel, and every man fled to his home. ²³ Jehoash king of Israel captured Amaziah king of Judah, the son of Joash, the son of Ahaziah, at Beth Shemesh. Then Jehoash brought him to Jerusalem and broke down the wall of Jerusalem from the Ephraim Gate to the Corner Gate—a section about four hundred cubits long. ²⁴ He took all the gold and silver and all the articles found in the temple of God that had been in the care of Obed-Edom, together with the palace treasures and the hostages, and returned to Samaria. . . .*

*²⁷ From the time that Amaziah turned away from following the LORD, they conspired against him in Jerusalem and he fled to Lachish, but they sent men after him to Lachish and killed him there. ²⁸ He was brought back by horse and was buried with his ancestors in the City of Judah.*

## Study Questions

1. To which of the people offering Amaziah advice did the young king listen? Why?

_____

_____

_____

_____

2. What advice did Amaziah ignore? Who did it come from? Why didn't he listen?

_____

_____

_____

_____

_____

_____

3. At what point could Amaziah have changed tacks, started listening, and changed the outcome he eventually faced?

_____

_____

_____

_____

_____

4. Do you think every leader has an opportunity to listen and change course for the better? Explain your answer.

_____

_____

_____

_____

_____

_____

_____

## ❸ Even Jesus Listened and Learned

Luke 2:41–52

*⁴¹ Every year Jesus' parents went to Jerusalem for the Festival of the Passover. ⁴² When he was twelve years old, they went up to the festival, according to the custom. ⁴³ After the festival was over, while his parents were returning home,*

*the boy Jesus stayed behind in Jerusalem, but they were unaware of it.*
*⁴⁴ Thinking he was in their company, they traveled on for a day. Then they began looking for him among their relatives and friends. ⁴⁵ When they did not find him, they went back to Jerusalem to look for him. ⁴⁶ After three days they found him in the temple courts, sitting among the teachers, listening to them and asking them questions. ⁴⁷ Everyone who heard him was amazed at his understanding and his answers. ⁴⁸ When his parents saw him, they were astonished. His mother said to him, "Son, why have you treated us like this? Your father and I have been anxiously searching for you."*

*⁴⁹ "Why were you searching for me?" he asked. "Didn't you know I had to be in my Father's house?" ⁵⁰ But they did not understand what he was saying to them.*

*⁵¹ Then he went down to Nazareth with them and was obedient to them. But his mother treasured all these things in her heart. ⁵² And Jesus grew in wisdom and stature, and in favor with God and man.*

## Study Questions

1. Why do you think Jesus' parents were surprised to find him listening to the teachers in the temple courts and asking them questions?

_____

_____

_____

_____

_____

_____

_____

2. What do you think Jesus' motivations were for doing what he did?

_____

_____

_____

_____

_____

3. What evidence can you find in the passage that Jesus was a learner?

_____

_____

_____

_____

_____

_____

# LEADERSHIP INSIGHT AND REFLECTION

Think about the motivation of each of the leaders in these passages. Write them here. Also note whether the leader was a good listener.

Samuel: _____

Eli: _____

Amaziah: _____

Jesus: _____

Now think about the outcome each leader experienced. Summarize those here:

Samuel: _____

Eli: _____

Amaziah: _____

Jesus: _____

What correlation is there between a leader's motives, his willingness to listen, and the outcome he experienced? What other factors come into play?

_____

_____

_____

_____

_____

_____

What observation can you make about listening leaders that could help you to improve your leadership?

_____

_____

_____

_____

_____

_____

_____

_____

_____

_____

_____

_____

# TAKING ACTION

Based on your analysis of the four leaders in the passages, what do you need to change in order to become a better listener?

_____

_____

_____

_____

_____

_____

_____

_____

_____

_____

_____

_____

_____

## What will you do about it?

# GROUP DISCUSSION QUESTIONS

1. The prophecy Samuel gave Eli came to be true; eventually, Eli's sons were killed (see 1 Samuel 4:11). Samuel went on to become one of the greatest prophets in Scripture. What was the difference between the way Samuel and Eli listened?

2. What causes leaders who once listened to stop listening, as was the case with Amaziah?

3. When Amaziah told the prophet to stop speaking and threatened to kill him, do you think the man should have continued to speak up anyway? Explain. What do you believe would have happened if he had kept speaking?

4. Did it surprise you that Jesus went to the temple courts to listen to the teachers? Explain your answer.

5. Luke writes of Jesus, "Everyone who heard him was amazed at his understanding and his answers" (2:47). What can you infer from this about the communication between Jesus and the teachers?

6. How would you rate yourself as a listener? Would others agree? Where do you most need to grow in this area?

7. What action do you believe God is asking you to take to become a better listener? When and how will you do it?

# PASSION

## Internal Combustion Creates
## Power and Motion

### THE QUALITY DEFINED

What one thing do a star baseball player, a successful entrepreneur, and a prolific artist all have in common? It's not the talent they possess; the talents necessary to succeed in each field are very different from each other. It's not opportunity; they certainly took various paths to get where they are. So what is the one trait that each of them must have to excel as much as they do in their respective field? Passion.

You've probably heard the saying, "Do what you love, and you'll never work a day in your life." I don't know if that's always true. Even the most heart-stirring career has elements of boredom or drudgery. But a passion for your work does give you something significant: the ability to achieve many more results, at a much higher level, than you would be able to do without it. Talent is not enough; passion is a difference-maker.

For leaders, passion is even more valuable because it's contagious. A leader who shows passion passes it on to followers. Passionate leaders also tend to attract new followers who already share their passion. And so passion builds, until the team is eagerly pursuing their dream together.

As a leader, the first question you must ask yourself is, "Do I have passion for what I'm doing?" If not, then it might be time to reassess your current role and duties. Or maybe find a way to relight or stoke the fire within by spending time with people of passion.

There is no substitute for passion. It is a spark to light a fire within. It's fuel for the will, keeping people going even when they're tired and tempted to quit. It is more powerful than circumstances, plowing through seeming impossibilities. If passion is not a quality in your life, you're in trouble as a leader. The truth is that you can never effectively lead something you don't care passionately about. You can't start or sustain a fire in your organization unless one is first burning within you.

# CASE STUDIES

Read these case studies from the Bible and answer the study questions that follow.

## 1 John the Baptist's Fire Is Evident to All

### Luke 3:1–18

*1 In the fifteenth year of the reign of Tiberius Caesar—when Pontius Pilate was governor of Judea, Herod tetrarch of Galilee, his brother Philip tetrarch of Iturea and Traconitis, and Lysanias tetrarch of Abilene— 2 during the high-priesthood of Annas and Caiaphas, the word of God came to John son of Zechariah in the wilderness. 3 He went into all the country around the Jordan, preaching a baptism of repentance for the forgiveness of sins. 4 As it is written in the book of the words of Isaiah the prophet:*

> *"A voice of one calling in the wilderness,*
> *'Prepare the way for the Lord,*
> *     make straight paths for him.*
> *5 Every valley shall be filled in,*
> *     every mountain and hill made low.*
> *The crooked roads shall become straight,*
> *     the rough ways smooth.*
> *6 And all people will see God's salvation.'"*

*7 John said to the crowds coming out to be baptized by him, "You brood of vipers! Who warned you to flee from the coming wrath? 8 Produce fruit in keeping with repentance. And do not begin to say to yourselves, 'We have Abraham as our father.' For I tell you that out of these stones God can raise up children for Abraham. ⁹ The ax is already at the root of the trees, and every tree that does not produce good fruit will be cut down and thrown into the fire."*

*¹⁰ "What should we do then?" the crowd asked.*

*¹¹ John answered, "Anyone who has two shirts should share with the one who has none, and anyone who has food should do the same."*

*¹² Even tax collectors came to be baptized. "Teacher," they asked, "what should we do?"*

*¹³ "Don't collect any more than you are required to," he told them.*

*¹⁴ Then some soldiers asked him, "And what should we do?"*

*He replied, "Don't extort money and don't accuse people falsely— be content with your pay."*

*¹⁵ The people were waiting expectantly and were all wondering in their hearts if John might possibly be the Messiah. ¹⁶ John answered them all, "I baptize you with water. But one who is more powerful than I will come, the straps of whose sandals I am not worthy to untie. He will baptize you with the Holy Spirit and fire. ¹⁷ His winnowing fork is in his hand to clear his threshing floor and to gather the wheat into his barn, but he will burn up the chaff with unquenchable fire." ¹⁸ And with many other words John exhorted the people and proclaimed the good news to them.*

## Study Questions

1. What would you say were the things John the Baptist was passionate about?

_____

_____

_____

_____

_____

_____

_____

_____

2. How much of his passion do you think came from his calling from God and how much from John himself?

_____

_____

_____

_____

_____

_____

3. How contagious was John's passion? Examine the passage for evidence that it spread to others and list some examples.

_____

_____

_____

_____

_____

_____

4. What role did John's method of communication play in the spread of his passion?

_____

_____

_____

_____

_____

_____

_____

_____

_____

## ② Whatever You Do . . .

### Colossians 3:1–17, 23–24

*¹ Since, then, you have been raised with Christ, set your hearts on things above, where Christ is, seated at the right hand of God. ² Set your minds on things above, not on earthly things. ³ For you died, and your life is now hidden with Christ in God. ⁴ When Christ, who is your life, appears, then you also will appear with him in glory.*

*⁵ Put to death, therefore, whatever belongs to your earthly nature: sexual immorality, impurity, lust, evil desires and greed, which is idolatry. ⁶ Because of these, the wrath of God is coming. ⁷ You used to walk in these ways, in the life you once lived. ⁸ But now you must also rid yourselves of all such things as these: anger, rage, malice, slander, and filthy language from your lips. ⁹ Do not lie to each other, since you have taken off your old self with its practices ¹⁰ and have put on the new self, which is being renewed in knowledge in the image of its Creator. ¹¹ Here there is no Gentile or Jew, circumcised or uncircumcised, barbarian, Scythian, slave or free, but Christ is all, and is in all.*

*¹² Therefore, as God's chosen people, holy and dearly loved, clothe yourselves with compassion, kindness, humility, gentleness and patience. ¹³ Bear with each other and forgive one another if any of you has a grievance against someone. Forgive as the Lord forgave you. ¹⁴ And over all these virtues put on love, which binds them all together in perfect unity.*

*¹⁵ Let the peace of Christ rule in your hearts, since as members of one body you were called to peace. And be thankful. ¹⁶ Let the message of Christ dwell among you richly as you teach and admonish one another with all wisdom through psalms, hymns, and songs from the Spirit, singing to God with gratitude in your hearts. ¹⁷ And whatever you do, whether in word or deed, do it all in the name of the Lord Jesus, giving thanks to God the Father through him. . . .*

*²³ Whatever you do, work at it with all your heart, as working for the Lord, not for human masters, ²⁴ since you know that you will receive an inheritance from the Lord as a reward. It is the Lord Christ you are serving.*

## Study Questions

1. Based on what Paul wrote to the Colossians in this passage, how important is it to be passionate about the right things?

_____

_____

_____

_____

2. What about the *way* we express passion? What guidelines did Paul give for how people should live and express themselves while being passionate?

_____

_____

_____

_____

_____

_____

3. The last part of the passage was directed specifically to slaves. What broader conclusions about work can you draw from Paul's admonition?

_____

_____

_____

_____

## ❸ The Cloud of Witnesses

### Hebrews 11:4–12, 22–34

*⁴ By faith Abel brought God a better offering than Cain did. By faith he was commended as righteous, when God spoke well of his offerings. And by faith Abel still speaks, even though he is dead.*

⁵ By faith Enoch was taken from this life, so that he did not experience death: "He could not be found, because God had taken him away." For before he was taken, he was commended as one who pleased God. ⁶ And without faith it is impossible to please God, because anyone who comes to him must believe that he exists and that he rewards those who earnestly seek him.

⁷ By faith Noah, when warned about things not yet seen, in holy fear built an ark to save his family. By his faith he condemned the world and became heir of the righteousness that is in keeping with faith.

⁸ By faith Abraham, when called to go to a place he would later receive as his inheritance, obeyed and went, even though he did not know where he was going. ⁹ By faith he made his home in the promised land like a stranger in a foreign country; he lived in tents, as did Isaac and Jacob, who were heirs with him of the same promise. ¹⁰ For he was looking forward to the city with foundations, whose architect and builder is God. ¹¹ And by faith even Sarah, who was past childbearing age, was enabled to bear children because she considered him faithful who had made the promise. ¹² And so from this one man, and he as good as dead, came descendants as numerous as the stars in the sky and as countless as the sand on the seashore. . . .

²² By faith Joseph, when his end was near, spoke about the exodus of the Israelites from Egypt and gave instructions concerning the burial of his bones.

²³ By faith Moses' parents hid him for three months after he was born, because they saw he was no ordinary child, and they were not afraid of the king's edict.

²⁴ By faith Moses, when he had grown up, refused to be known as the son of Pharaoh's daughter. ²⁵ He chose to be mistreated along with the people of God rather than to enjoy the fleeting pleasures of sin. ²⁶ He regarded disgrace for the sake of Christ as of greater value than the treasures of Egypt, because he was looking ahead to his reward. ²⁷ By faith he left Egypt, not fearing the king's anger; he persevered because he saw him who is invisible. ²⁸ By faith he kept the Passover and the application of blood, so that the destroyer of the firstborn would not touch the firstborn of Israel.

²⁹ By faith the people passed through the Red Sea as on dry land; but when the Egyptians tried to do so, they were drowned.

³⁰ By faith the walls of Jericho fell, after the army had marched around them for seven days.

*31 By faith the prostitute Rahab, because she welcomed the spies, was not killed with those who were disobedient.*

*32 And what more shall I say? I do not have time to tell about Gideon, Barak, Samson and Jephthah, about David and Samuel and the prophets, 33 who through faith conquered kingdoms, administered justice, and gained what was promised; who shut the mouths of lions, 34 quenched the fury of the flames, and escaped the edge of the sword; whose weakness was turned to strength; and who became powerful in battle and routed foreign armies.*

## Hebrews 12:1–3

*1 Therefore, since we are surrounded by such a great cloud of witnesses, let us throw off everything that hinders and the sin that so easily entangles. And let us run with perseverance the race marked out for us, 2 fixing our eyes on Jesus, the pioneer and perfecter of faith. For the joy set before him he endured the cross, scorning its shame, and sat down at the right hand of the throne of God. 3 Consider him who endured such opposition from sinners, so that you will not grow weary and lose heart.*

## Study Questions

1. It's clear from this passage the men and women mentioned were passionate about their faith. How do you believe that passion helped them to deal with adversity?

2. Many of the people listed in this passage reached the heights of their professions. Based on what you know about them, speculate about how their passions for faith and their professional work related to one another. How did they pursue both?

_____

_____

_____

_____

_____

_____

_____

_____

_____

3. What do you think the writer of Hebrews meant when he wrote, "Let us run with perseverance the race marked out for us" (12:1)? What are the implications of that statement for anyone who follows Christ? And how might passion come into play?

_____

_____

_____

_____

_____

_____

_____

_____

_____

_____

_____

# LEADERSHIP INSIGHT AND REFLECTION

John the Baptist's job and calling appeared to be one and the same. That was also true for several of the people mentioned in Hebrews, though not all of them. And the Colossians passage indicates any work can and perhaps should be done in the spirit of doing it for God. Knowing all that, how do you know what race has been marked out for you? How do work, faith, and calling intersect and interact for you?

_____

_____

_____

_____

_____

_____

_____

_____

How does passion come into play in each of those three areas?

_____

_____

_____

_____

_____

_____

When you read the phrase "throw off everything that hinders and the sin that so easily entangles" (Hebrews 12:1), what issues come to mind for you personally? What threatens you from running the race marked out for you?

_____

_____

_____

_____

_____

_____

_____

_____

# TAKING ACTION

Where do you need to grow when it comes to passion to become a better follower of Christ? Where do you need to increase and demonstrate your passion to become a better leader?

_____

_____

_____

_____

_____

_____

_____

What will you do to fire your passion? How will you sustain it?

_____

_____

_____

_____

_____

_____

_____

_____

_____

# GROUP DISCUSSION QUESTIONS

1. How difficult do you think it was for John the Baptist to preach to the people of Israel knowing that he was only the forerunner of someone so much greater than he was? Would you think it would decrease or increase his passion?

2. In the runup to Paul's admonition to "do it all in the name of the Lord Jesus" (Colossians 3:17), why do you think he told people to avoid specific examples of immoral behavior and to embrace behaviors that honor Christ? How do the ideas of work and morality relate to one another?

3. When you read the passage in Hebrews 11 naming some of the greatest examples of faith, did you relate to any of them? If so, who and why? If not, why not?

4. What are you most passionate about in your life?

5. How does that passion relate to your faith, your work, your calling, and your leadership?

6. If there were a way to align all those things with your passion, what would you be doing?

7. What changes would you have to make in your life to achieve that? Would it be worth it? Would it honor God? What's keeping you from pursuing it?

# POSITIVE ATTITUDE

## If You Believe You Can, You Can

### THE QUALITY DEFINED

If you set out to climb a mountain, and you have a choice between two experienced and capable guides, which of these would you choose? Guide number one is smiling and appears eager to get started on the climb. He also expresses absolute confidence that the group will reach the summit. Guide number two appears critical, uncertain, perhaps even worried. He seems hesitant to move. And he talks more about the obstacles ahead than about the summit beyond.

You'd choose guide number one, right? After all, we all prefer to follow someone who believes he can take us where we want to go, especially when the road ahead looks challenging. A positive leader communicates confidence, hope, and excitement. And all of this encourages followers to keep going, even when the going gets tough.

Your attitude as a leader is a choice, and it affects more than your own actions; it has a significant impact on the attitudes and actions of your followers. Leaders with a positive attitude intentionally steer their focus, their beliefs, and their assumptions in a positive direction. They focus more on being grateful for positive circumstances than on complaining about negative ones. They choose to believe that outcomes will be positive in the end. And they assume the best motives in others.

A positive attitude can make the difference between winning the game and losing, between reaching the summit and turning back, and between achieving your organization's goals and falling short. Be the confident guide, and your people will want to follow you. They will imitate your example and press on with you even when the going gets tough. Attitude is contagious. Cultivate the right one, and that positivity will spread, taking you and your people as far as you can imagine going.

# CASE STUDIES

Read these case studies from the Bible and answer the study questions that follow.

## ① A Negative Attitude Dooms a Generation

### Numbers 13:1–2, 17–33

¹ *The LORD said to Moses,* ² *"Send some men to explore the land of Canaan, which I am giving to the Israelites. From each ancestral tribe send one of its leaders."...*

¹⁷ *When Moses sent them to explore Canaan, he said, "Go up through the Negev and on into the hill country.* ¹⁸ *See what the land is like and whether the people who live there are strong or weak, few or many.* ¹⁹ *What kind of land do they live in? Is it good or bad? What kind of towns do they live in? Are they unwalled or fortified?* ²⁰ *How is the soil? Is it fertile or poor? Are there trees in it or not? Do your best to bring back some of the fruit of the land."* *(It was the season for the first ripe grapes.)*

²¹ *So they went up and explored the land from the Desert of Zin as far as Rehob, toward Lebo Hamath.* ²² *They went up through the Negev and came to Hebron, where Ahiman, Sheshai and Talmai, the descendants of Anak, lived. (Hebron had been built seven years before Zoan in Egypt.)* ²³ *When they reached the Valley of Eshkol, they cut off a branch bearing a single cluster of grapes. Two of them carried it on a pole between them, along with some pomegranates and figs.* ²⁴ *That place was called the Valley of Eshkol because*

*of the cluster of grapes the Israelites cut off there. ²⁵ At the end of forty days they returned from exploring the land.*

*²⁶ They came back to Moses and Aaron and the whole Israelite community at Kadesh in the Desert of Paran. There they reported to them and to the whole assembly and showed them the fruit of the land. ²⁷ They gave Moses this account: "We went into the land to which you sent us, and it does flow with milk and honey! Here is its fruit. ²⁸ But the people who live there are powerful, and the cities are fortified and very large. We even saw descendants of Anak there. ²⁹ The Amalekites live in the Negev; the Hittites, Jebusites and Amorites live in the hill country; and the Canaanites live near the sea and along the Jordan."*

*³⁰ Then Caleb silenced the people before Moses and said, "We should go up and take possession of the land, for we can certainly do it."*

*³¹ But the men who had gone up with him said, "We can't attack those people; they are stronger than we are." ³² And they spread among the Israelites a bad report about the land they had explored. They said, "The land we explored devours those living in it. All the people we saw there are of great size. ³³ We saw the Nephilim there (the descendants of Anak come from the Nephilim). We seemed like grasshoppers in our own eyes, and we looked the same to them."*

## Numbers 14:1–4, 26–33

*¹ That night all the members of the community raised their voices and wept aloud. ² All the Israelites grumbled against Moses and Aaron, and the whole assembly said to them, "If only we had died in Egypt! Or in this wilderness! ³ Why is the Lᴏʀᴅ bringing us to this land only to let us fall by the sword? Our wives and children will be taken as plunder. Wouldn't it be better for us to go back to Egypt?" ⁴ And they said to each other, "We should choose a leader and go back to Egypt.". . .*

*²⁶ The Lᴏʀᴅ said to Moses and Aaron: ²⁷ "How long will this wicked community grumble against me? I have heard the complaints of these grumbling Israelites. ²⁸ So tell them, 'As surely as I live, declares the Lᴏʀᴅ, I will do to you the very thing I heard you say: ²⁹ In this wilderness your bodies will fall—every one of you twenty years old or more who was counted in the census and who has grumbled against me. ³⁰ Not one of you will enter the land I swore with uplifted hand to make your home, except Caleb son of Jephunneh and Joshua son of Nun. ³¹ As for your children that you said would be taken as plunder, I will bring them in to enjoy the land you have rejected. ³² But as for you, your bodies will fall in this wilderness. ³³ Your children will be shepherds here for forty years, suffering for your unfaithfulness, until the last of your bodies lies in the wilderness."*

## Study Questions

1. Why did ten of the twelve spies speak negatively about the land of Canaan?

   _____

   _____

   _____

   _____

   _____

2. Based on the passage, what part of the negative spies' report was factual and what part was not? Why do you think they embellished their report?

   _____

   _____

   _____

   _____

   _____

3. Why couldn't Moses, Aaron, Caleb, and Joshua stop the spread of negative thinking?

   _____

   _____

   _____

   _____

   _____

4. What do you think would have happened if more of the spies had spoken positively about the promised land? What do you think would have turned the tide?

_____

_____

_____

_____

## ② Isaiah Paints a Picture of Hope

Isaiah 40:6–15, 21–26, 28–31

⁶ A voice says, "Cry out."
   And I said, "What shall I cry?"

"All people are like grass,
   and all their faithfulness is like the flowers of the field.
⁷ The grass withers and the flowers fall,
   because the breath of the LORD blows on them.
   Surely the people are grass.
⁸ The grass withers and the flowers fall,
   but the word of our God endures forever."

⁹ You who bring good news to Zion,
   go up on a high mountain.
You who bring good news to Jerusalem,
   lift up your voice with a shout,
lift it up, do not be afraid;
   say to the towns of Judah,
   "Here is your God!"
¹⁰ See, the Sovereign LORD comes with power,
   and he rules with a mighty arm.
See, his reward is with him,
   and his recompense accompanies him.

¹¹ He tends his flock like a shepherd:
    He gathers the lambs in his arms
and carries them close to his heart;
    he gently leads those that have young.

¹² Who has measured the waters in the hollow of his hand,
    or with the breadth of his hand marked off the heavens?
Who has held the dust of the earth in a basket,
    or weighed the mountains on the scales
    and the hills in a balance?
¹³ Who can fathom the Spirit of the Lord,
    or instruct the Lord as his counselor?
¹⁴ Whom did the Lord consult to enlighten him,
    and who taught him the right way?
Who was it that taught him knowledge,
    or showed him the path of understanding?

¹⁵ Surely the nations are like a drop in a bucket;
    they are regarded as dust on the scales;
    he weighs the islands as though they were fine dust. . . .

²¹ Do you not know?
    Have you not heard?
Has it not been told you from the beginning?
    Have you not understood since the earth was founded?
²² He sits enthroned above the circle of the earth,
    and its people are like grasshoppers.
He stretches out the heavens like a canopy,
    and spreads them out like a tent to live in.
²³ He brings princes to naught
    and reduces the rulers of this world to nothing.
²⁴ No sooner are they planted,
    no sooner are they sown,
    no sooner do they take root in the ground,
than he blows on them and they wither,
    and a whirlwind sweeps them away like chaff.

*25 "To whom will you compare me?*
*Or who is my equal?" says the Holy One.*
*26 Lift up your eyes and look to the heavens:*
*Who created all these?*
*He who brings out the starry host one by one*
*and calls forth each of them by name.*
*Because of his great power and mighty strength,*
*not one of them is missing. . . .*

*28 Do you not know?*
*Have you not heard?*
*The LORD is the everlasting God,*
*the Creator of the ends of the earth.*
*He will not grow tired or weary,*
*and his understanding no one can fathom.*
*29 He gives strength to the weary*
*and increases the power of the weak.*
*30 Even youths grow tired and weary,*
*and young men stumble and fall;*
*31 but those who hope in the LORD*
*will renew their strength.*
*They will soar on wings like eagles;*
*they will run and not grow weary,*
*they will walk and not be faint.*

## Study Questions

1. What negatives that human beings face are described in this passage? List them.

2. What positives are listed that counter these negative experiences?

_____

_____

_____

_____

3. What is the source of those positives? And why are human beings granted them?

_____

_____

_____

_____

_____

_____

4. Which do you think outweighs the other: the positive or the negative? Why?

_____

_____

_____

_____

_____

_____

## ❸ Jesus on Asking and Receiving

### Matthew 7:7–12

*7 "Ask and it will be given to you; seek and you will find; knock and the door will be opened to you. 8 For everyone who asks receives; the one who seeks finds; and to the one who knocks, the door will be opened.*

*9 "Which of you, if your son asks for bread, will give him a stone? 10 Or if he asks for a fish, will give him a snake? 11 If you, then, though you are evil, know how to give good gifts to your children, how much more will your Father in heaven give good gifts to those who ask him! ¹² So in everything, do to others what you would have them do to you, for this sums up the Law and the Prophets."*

## Study Questions

1. How would you say that Jesus characterizes God in this passage on prayer? Describe God's attitude, character, and personality.

2. What positive outcomes does God want for those who interact with him?

3. What might Jesus say to any follower of his who possesses a negative attitude?

# LEADERSHIP INSIGHT AND REFLECTION

Where did the ten negative spies place their hope? And how did that impact their attitude?

_____

_____

_____

_____

_____

_____

_____

How does Isaiah's description of God and Jesus' depiction of him differ from the way you think of God?

_____

_____

_____

_____

_____

_____

_____

_____

If you were to fully embrace Jesus' description of God and believe it to the depths of your soul, how would it change you? How would it impact your leadership?

_____

_____

_____

_____

_____

_____

_____

# TAKING ACTION

How would you rate your attitude on a scale of 1 (negative) to 10 (positive)? _____

Where specifically is your attitude less positive than it could or should be?

_____

_____

_____

_____

_____

_____

_____

_____

How can you apply the insights about God from this lesson to your attitude to make you a more positive person and leader? What must you do?

_____

_____

_____

_____

_____

_____

_____

# GROUP DISCUSSION QUESTIONS

1. If you had been one of the twelve spies, how do you think you would have felt going into Canaan to spy it out?

2. God told Moses to send the spies into the promised land, so it was right for him to obey. But do you think it was a mistake for Moses to ask them to examine the people's strength and number, the fortification of their towns, and the desirability of the land?

3. What specific phrases in the Isaiah passage jump out at you? Explain why they do and what they mean to you.

4. Do you find it easy or difficult to believe that everyone who asks God will receive? Explain.

5. When you face difficult circumstances or have a negative frame of mind, how do you typically deal with it? How often do you think about the promises of God and his character to counter it? Explain.

6. What was your greatest takeaway about attitude from this lesson?

7. What action do you believe God is asking you to take when it comes to your attitude to make you a better person and leader? What action will you take?

# LESSON 14

# PROBLEM SOLVING

## You Can't Let Your Problems Be a Problem

### THE QUALITY DEFINED

"In this world you will have trouble," said Jesus. "But take heart! I have overcome the world" (John 16:33). As we go through life here on earth, trouble is a given. Problems are unavoidable, but they don't have to be insurmountable. Problems become a problem only when we let them. It's all a matter of perspective. As author Robert Kiyosaki said, "Inside of every problem lies an opportunity."

Problems are everywhere, and they can have a negative effect on followers as well as the leader. Leaders have a responsibility to help their people solve problems as quickly and effectively as possible. So how do you "take heart" in the face of problems? The first step is to admit that problems will come. Many people expect—or at least hope for—smooth sailing. Once a leader has accepted that rough water is inevitable, they are able to anticipate and prepare for it, not in a negative way, but realistically. Leaders can handle anything that comes when they expect the best but plan for the worst.

Problems are simply obstacles in the path toward a goal. It's easy to let them block the view of the finish line. Effective leaders look past the problems and keep their minds on the goal and the big picture. This combats hopelessness and powerlessness. It also can reveal the way past the obstacle, especially when people search for solutions creatively and think outside the box.

Every problem introduces you to yourself. It reveals how you think and what you're made of. Do you stop or turn back when confronted with an obstacle? Or find a way over, under, or around it? Getting past problems is a crucial part of achieving your goals. Every time you choose to see beyond a problem and think creatively until you find its solution, you not only get closer to your objective, you also increase your skill as a problem solver.

# CASE STUDIES

Read these case studies from the Bible and answer the study questions that follow.

## ① The Shunammite and Elisha

### 2 Kings 4:8–37

*8 One day Elisha went to Shunem. And a well-to-do woman was there, who urged him to stay for a meal. So whenever he came by, he stopped there to eat. 9 She said to her husband, "I know that this man who often comes our way is a holy man of God. 10 Let's make a small room on the roof and put in it a bed and a table, a chair and a lamp for him. Then he can stay there whenever he comes to us."*

*11 One day when Elisha came, he went up to his room and lay down there. 12 He said to his servant Gehazi, "Call the Shunammite." So he called her, and she stood before him. 13 Elisha said to him, "Tell her, 'You have gone to all this trouble for us. Now what can be done for you? Can we speak on your behalf to the king or the commander of the army?'"*

*She replied, "I have a home among my own people."*

*14 "What can be done for her?" Elisha asked.*

*Gehazi said, "She has no son, and her husband is old."*

*15 Then Elisha said, "Call her." So he called her, and she stood in the doorway. 16 "About this time next year," Elisha said, "you will hold a son in your arms."*

*"No, my lord!" she objected. "Please, man of God, don't mislead your servant!"*

*17 But the woman became pregnant, and the next year about that same time she gave birth to a son, just as Elisha had told her.*

*18 The child grew, and one day he went out to his father, who was with the reapers. 19 He said to his father, "My head! My head!"*

*His father told a servant, "Carry him to his mother." 20 After the servant had lifted him up and carried him to his mother, the boy sat on her lap until noon, and then he died. 21 She went up and laid him on the bed of the man of God, then shut the door and went out.*

*22 She called her husband and said, "Please send me one of the servants and a donkey so I can go to the man of God quickly and return."*

*23 "Why go to him today?" he asked. "It's not the New Moon or the Sabbath."*

*"That's all right," she said.*

*24 She saddled the donkey and said to her servant, "Lead on; don't slow down for me unless I tell you." 25 So she set out and came to the man of God at Mount Carmel.*

*When he saw her in the distance, the man of God said to his servant Gehazi, "Look! There's the Shunammite! 26 Run to meet her and ask her, 'Are you all right? Is your husband all right? Is your child all right?'"*

*"Everything is all right," she said.*

*27 When she reached the man of God at the mountain, she took hold of his feet. Gehazi came over to push her away, but the man of God said, "Leave her alone! She is in bitter distress, but the Lord has hidden it from me and has not told me why."*

*28 "Did I ask you for a son, my lord?" she said. "Didn't I tell you, 'Don't raise my hopes'?"*

*29 Elisha said to Gehazi, "Tuck your cloak into your belt, take my staff in your hand and run. Don't greet anyone you meet, and if anyone greets you, do not answer. Lay my staff on the boy's face."*

*30 But the child's mother said, "As surely as the Lord lives and as you live, I will not leave you." So he got up and followed her.*

*31 Gehazi went on ahead and laid the staff on the boy's face, but there was no sound or response. So Gehazi went back to meet Elisha and told him, "The boy has not awakened."*

*32 When Elisha reached the house, there was the boy lying dead on his couch. 33 He went in, shut the door on the two of them and prayed to the Lord.*

*34 Then he got on the bed and lay on the boy, mouth to mouth, eyes to eyes, hands to hands. As he stretched himself out on him, the boy's body grew warm. 35 Elisha turned away and walked back and forth in the room and then got on the bed and stretched out on him once more. The boy sneezed seven times and opened his eyes.*

*36 Elisha summoned Gehazi and said, "Call the Shunammite." And he did. When she came, he said, "Take your son." 37 She came in, fell at his feet and bowed to the ground. Then she took her son and went out.*

## Study Questions

1. What do you think motivated the Shunammite woman to initially care for Elisha?

2. Why do you think Elisha asked his servant Gehazi, "What can be done for her" (verse 14)?

3. Why do you think the Shunammite told Gehazi, "Everything is all right" (verse 26), but then grabbed the feet of Elisha and wouldn't let go?

4. How would you describe the Shunammite's handling of her son's death? How would you describe Elisha's response? What do their actions reveal about them?

_____

_____

_____

_____

_____

_____

## ❷ Esther and Mordecai Follow Through

### Esther 8:1–14

*¹ That same day King Xerxes gave Queen Esther the estate of Haman, the enemy of the Jews. And Mordecai came into the presence of the king, for Esther had told how he was related to her. ² The king took off his signet ring, which he had reclaimed from Haman, and presented it to Mordecai. And Esther appointed him over Haman's estate.*

*³ Esther again pleaded with the king, falling at his feet and weeping. She begged him to put an end to the evil plan of Haman the Agagite, which he had devised against the Jews. ⁴ Then the king extended the gold scepter to Esther and she arose and stood before him.*

*⁵ "If it pleases the king," she said, "and if he regards me with favor and thinks it the right thing to do, and if he is pleased with me, let an order be written overruling the dispatches that Haman son of Hammedatha, the Agagite, devised and wrote to destroy the Jews in all the king's provinces. ⁶ For how can I bear to see disaster fall on my people? How can I bear to see the destruction of my family?"*

*⁷ King Xerxes replied to Queen Esther and to Mordecai the Jew, "Because Haman attacked the Jews, I have given his estate to Esther, and they have impaled him on the pole he set up. ⁸ Now write another decree in the king's name in behalf of the Jews as seems best to you, and seal it with the king's signet ring—for no document written in the king's name and sealed with his ring can be revoked."*

*⁹ At once the royal secretaries were summoned—on the twenty-third day of the third month, the month of Sivan. They wrote out all Mordecai's orders to the Jews, and to the satraps, governors and nobles of the 127 provinces stretching from India to Cush. These orders were written in the script of each province and the language of each people and also to the Jews in their own script and language. ¹⁰ Mordecai wrote in the name of King Xerxes, sealed the dispatches with the king's signet ring, and sent them by mounted couriers, who rode fast horses especially bred for the king.*

*¹¹ The king's edict granted the Jews in every city the right to assemble and protect themselves; to destroy, kill and annihilate the armed men of any nationality or province who might attack them and their women and children, and to plunder the property of their enemies. ¹² The day appointed for the Jews to do this in all the provinces of King Xerxes was the thirteenth day of the twelfth month, the month of Adar. ¹³ A copy of the text of the edict was to be issued as law in every province and made known to the people of every nationality so that the Jews would be ready on that day to avenge themselves on their enemies.*

*¹⁴ The couriers, riding the royal horses, went out, spurred on by the king's command, and the edict was issued in the citadel of Susa.*

## Study Questions

1. In lesson 6, you read how Esther approached King Xerxes and exposed the plot of Haman, who was then executed by the king's order. Why didn't that solve the problem exposed by Mordecai and Esther?

_____

_____

_____

_____

_____

2. Based on what was described in the edict, how thorough was Mordecai's solution to the problem? Describe the contingencies he took into account.

_____

_____

_____

_____

_____

3. What was King Xerxes' contribution to solving this problem?

_____

_____

_____

_____

_____

4. How much of a team effort was needed in solving the problem the Jews faced? Could it have been solved without Xerxes, Esther, or Mordecai? Explain.

_____

_____

_____

_____

_____

## ❸ A Creative Solution

### Mark 5:21–34

*²¹ When Jesus had again crossed over by boat to the other side of the lake, a large crowd gathered around him while he was by the lake. ²² Then one of the synagogue leaders, named Jairus, came, and when he saw Jesus, he fell* at his feet. [23] He pleaded earnestly with him, "My little daughter is dying. Please come and put your hands on her so that she will be healed and live." [24] So Jesus went with him.

A large crowd followed and pressed around him. [25] And a woman was there who had been subject to bleeding for twelve years. [26] She had suffered a great deal under the care of many doctors and had spent all she had, yet instead of getting better she grew worse. [27] When she heard about Jesus, she came up behind him in the crowd and touched his cloak, [28] because she thought, "If I just touch his clothes, I will be healed." [29] Immediately her bleeding stopped and she felt in her body that she was freed from her suffering.

[30] At once Jesus realized that power had gone out from him. He turned around in the crowd and asked, "Who touched my clothes?"

[31] "You see the people crowding against you," his disciples answered, "and yet you can ask, 'Who touched me?'"

[32] But Jesus kept looking around to see who had done it. [33] Then the woman, knowing what had happened to her, came and fell at his feet and, trembling with fear, told him the whole truth. [34] He said to her, "Daughter, your faith has healed you. Go in peace and be freed from your suffering."

## Study Questions

1. What do you imagine the woman's mindset was after twelve years of suffering, spending all of her money on doctors, and getting worse instead of better?

_____

_____

_____

_____

_____

_____

2. Do you think her decision to try to touch Jesus' clothes was something
   she had traveled to that location specifically to do, or was it an opportunity that presented itself unexpectedly in the moment and she seized it?
   Explain your answer.

   _____

   _____

   _____

   _____

   _____

   _____

3. Why do you think the woman was initially reluctant to reveal herself as the
   person who touched Jesus and received the power that had gone out of him?

   _____

   _____

   _____

   _____

   _____

   _____

4. What can be learned about problem solving from the actions of the woman?
   What can you learn about God from Jesus' response to her?

   _____

   _____

   _____

   _____

   _____

   _____

   _____

   _____

   _____

# LEADERSHIP INSIGHT AND REFLECTION

Based on the examples in these passages, what are the roles of awareness, courage, motivation, experience, creativity, strategic thinking, follow-through, and perseverance when it comes to problem solving? What other important factors would you include?

_____

_____

_____

_____

_____

_____

_____

_____

_____

_____

_____

_____

In which of those areas are you strong? How could you leverage that strength to become a better problem solver?

_____

_____

_____

_____

_____

_____

In which area are you weak? How could you improve in that area?

_____

_____

_____

_____

_____

_____

# TAKING ACTION

Where does God want you to grow in order to become a better problem solver?

_____

_____

_____

_____

_____

_____

_____

_____

How would that growth help you to become a better leader?

_____

_____

_____

_____

_____

_____

What action will you take immediately to start that growth process? How long will you attempt to sustain it?

_____

_____

_____

_____

_____

_____

_____

_____

_____

_____

# GROUP DISCUSSION QUESTIONS

1. How many solutions did Elisha attempt before succeeding in raising the Shunammite woman's son from the dead? Why do you think it required that many?

2. In your opinion, who was the better problem solver: the Shunammite woman or Elisha? Explain.

3. Who showed the greater leadership in the Esther passage: Xerxes, Esther, or Mordecai? Explain your answer.

4. Why do you think Jesus knew power had gone out from him, yet he had to ask who had touched him?

5. Two of these passages included supernatural solutions to problems where God intervened. When you face a problem, at what point, if any, do you appeal to God for help? What do you expect from him?

6. When solving problems as a leader, what do you consider to be your part, your team's part, and God's part?

7. Where do you need to improve most as a problem solver? What action do you believe God is asking you to take to make this improvement? When and how will you do it?

# RELATIONSHIPS

## If You Get Along, They'll Go Along

## THE QUALITY DEFINED

What is one big difference between a boss and an effective leader? With the boss, people follow because they have to. With a good leader, people follow because they want to. And it's a fact that followers are more likely to give their best when they want to, instead of when they feel forced or obligated to. Good relationships are the foundation of leadership that works.

Humans are relational beings. We are designed to connect, and life is only truly fulfilling in the context of relationships. This is true in leadership as well. If you simply order people around with no attempt to connect with them, they might meet the requirements of the job, but they will not contribute much more than the bare minimum of their effort. An organization led by a leader who has no people skills will not reach its full potential. In contrast, good relationships between all of the players can take an organization from good to great.

People truly do want to go along with those they get along with. So how do leaders develop people skills and connect with followers? They use their head, have a heart, and extend a hand.

They are using their heads when they get to know people to understand what matters to them and what motivates them. They take the time to ask questions and listen to their answers. They have a heart by treating people as individual human beings, not just team members or employees. They care, show empathy, and help to provide an environment where they can thrive and enjoy what they do. When a leader does those two things, lending a hand comes naturally. When people get their needs met first, they're much more likely to give back. Effective leaders give first because they care about their people and want to help them.

Some of us are more naturally relational than others, but people skills can definitely be learned. If you focus on leading with your head, your heart, and your hand, you will develop more fulfilling relationships, and your leadership and influence will grow.

# CASE STUDIES

Read these case studies from the Bible and answer the study questions that follow.

## ① Jacob Deceives Isaac

### Genesis 27:1–45

[1] When Isaac was old and his eyes were so weak that he could no longer see, he called for Esau his older son and said to him, "My son."

"Here I am," he answered.

[2] Isaac said, "I am now an old man and don't know the day of my death. [3] Now then, get your equipment—your quiver and bow—and go out to the open country to hunt some wild game for me. [4] Prepare me the kind of tasty food I like and bring it to me to eat, so that I may give you my blessing before I die."

[5] Now Rebekah was listening as Isaac spoke to his son Esau. When Esau left for the open country to hunt game and bring it back, [6] Rebekah said to her son Jacob, "Look, I overheard your father say to your brother Esau, [7] 'Bring me some game and prepare me some tasty food to eat, so that I may give you my blessing in the presence of the LORD before I die.' [8] Now, my son,

*listen carefully and do what I tell you: ⁹ Go out to the flock and bring me two choice young goats, so I can prepare some tasty food for your father, just the way he likes it. ¹⁰ Then take it to your father to eat, so that he may give you his blessing before he dies."*

*¹¹ Jacob said to Rebekah his mother, "But my brother Esau is a hairy man while I have smooth skin. ¹² What if my father touches me? I would appear to be tricking him and would bring down a curse on myself rather than a blessing."*

*¹³ His mother said to him, "My son, let the curse fall on me. Just do what I say; go and get them for me."*

*¹⁴ So he went and got them and brought them to his mother, and she prepared some tasty food, just the way his father liked it. ¹⁵ Then Rebekah took the best clothes of Esau her older son, which she had in the house, and put them on her younger son Jacob. ¹⁶ She also covered his hands and the smooth part of his neck with the goatskins. ¹⁷ Then she handed to her son Jacob the tasty food and the bread she had made.*

*¹⁸ He went to his father and said, "My father."*

*"Yes, my son," he answered. "Who is it?"*

*¹⁹ Jacob said to his father, "I am Esau your firstborn. I have done as you told me. Please sit up and eat some of my game, so that you may give me your blessing."*

*²⁰ Isaac asked his son, "How did you find it so quickly, my son?"*

*"The LORD your God gave me success," he replied.*

*²¹ Then Isaac said to Jacob, "Come near so I can touch you, my son, to know whether you really are my son Esau or not."*

*²² Jacob went close to his father Isaac, who touched him and said, "The voice is the voice of Jacob, but the hands are the hands of Esau." ²³ He did not recognize him, for his hands were hairy like those of his brother Esau; so he proceeded to bless him. ²⁴ "Are you really my son Esau?" he asked.*

*"I am," he replied.*

*²⁵ Then he said, "My son, bring me some of your game to eat, so that I may give you my blessing."*

*Jacob brought it to him and he ate; and he brought some wine and he drank. ²⁶ Then his father Isaac said to him, "Come here, my son, and kiss me."*

*27 So he went to him and kissed him. When Isaac caught the smell of his clothes, he blessed him and said,*

> *"Ah, the smell of my son*
> *is like the smell of a field*
> *that the Lord has blessed.*
> *28 May God give you heaven's dew*
> *and earth's richness—*
> *an abundance of grain and new wine.*
> *29 May nations serve you*
> *and peoples bow down to you.*
> *Be lord over your brothers,*
> *and may the sons of your mother bow down to you.*
> *May those who curse you be cursed*
> *and those who bless you be blessed."*

*30 After Isaac finished blessing him, and Jacob had scarcely left his father's presence, his brother Esau came in from hunting. 31 He too prepared some tasty food and brought it to his father. Then he said to him, "My father, please sit up and eat some of my game, so that you may give me your blessing."*

*32 His father Isaac asked him, "Who are you?"*

*"I am your son," he answered, "your firstborn, Esau."*

*33 Isaac trembled violently and said, "Who was it, then, that hunted game and brought it to me? I ate it just before you came and I blessed him—and indeed he will be blessed!"*

*34 When Esau heard his father's words, he burst out with a loud and bitter cry and said to his father, "Bless me—me too, my father!"*

*35 But he said, "Your brother came deceitfully and took your blessing."*

*36 Esau said, "Isn't he rightly named Jacob? This is the second time he has taken advantage of me: He took my birthright, and now he's taken my blessing!" Then he asked, "Haven't you reserved any blessing for me?"*

*37 Isaac answered Esau, "I have made him lord over you and have made all his relatives his servants, and I have sustained him with grain and new wine. So what can I possibly do for you, my son?"*

<sup>38</sup> *Esau said to his father, "Do you have only one blessing, my father? Bless me too, my father!" Then Esau wept aloud.*
   <sup>39</sup> *His father Isaac answered him,*

> *"Your dwelling will be*
>       *away from the earth's richness,*
>       *away from the dew of heaven above.*
> <sup>40</sup> *You will live by the sword*
>       *and you will serve your brother.*
> *But when you grow restless,*
>       *you will throw his yoke*
>       *from off your neck."*

<sup>41</sup> *Esau held a grudge against Jacob because of the blessing his father had given him. He said to himself, "The days of mourning for my father are near; then I will kill my brother Jacob."*
   <sup>42</sup> *When Rebekah was told what her older son Esau had said, she sent for her younger son Jacob and said to him, "Your brother Esau is planning to avenge himself by killing you.* <sup>43</sup> *Now then, my son, do what I say: Flee at once to my brother Laban in Harran.* <sup>44</sup> *Stay with him for a while until your brother's fury subsides.* <sup>45</sup> *When your brother is no longer angry with you and forgets what you did to him, I'll send word for you to come back from there. Why should I lose both of you in one day?"*

## Study Questions

1. How did Jacob view Esau?

2. Why did Rebekah instigate Jacob's deception? Do you think it was because the Lord had told her the older twin would serve the younger (see Genesis 25:23), because she loved Jacob more (see Genesis 25:28), or for some other reason?

_____

_____

_____

_____

3. What impact did the deception have on their family? How did it affect each person?

_____

_____

_____

_____

_____

## ② The Queen of Sheba Visits Solomon

### 1 Kings 10:1–10, 13

[1] *When the queen of Sheba heard about the fame of Solomon and his relationship to the LORD, she came to test Solomon with hard questions.* [2] *Arriving at Jerusalem with a very great caravan—with camels carrying spices, large quantities of gold, and precious stones—she came to Solomon and talked with him about all that she had on her mind.* [3] *Solomon answered all her questions; nothing was too hard for the king to explain to her.* [4] *When the queen of Sheba saw all the wisdom of Solomon and the palace he had built,* [5] *the food on his table, the seating of his officials, the attending servants in their robes, his cupbearers, and the burnt offerings he made at the temple of the LORD, she was overwhelmed.*

*⁶ She said to the king, "The report I heard in my own country about your achievements and your wisdom is true. ⁷ But I did not believe these things until I came and saw with my own eyes. Indeed, not even half was told me; in wisdom and wealth you have far exceeded the report I heard. ⁸ How happy your people must be! How happy your officials, who continually stand before you and hear your wisdom! ⁹ Praise be to the Lord your God, who has delighted in you and placed you on the throne of Israel. Because of the Lord's eternal love for Israel, he has made you king to maintain justice and righteousness."*

*¹⁰ And she gave the king 120 talents of gold, large quantities of spices, and precious stones. Never again were so many spices brought in as those the queen of Sheba gave to King Solomon. . . .*

*¹³ King Solomon gave the queen of Sheba all she desired and asked for, besides what he had given her out of his royal bounty. Then she left and returned with her retinue to her own country.*

## Study Questions

1. Why do you think the queen of Sheba traveled all the way to King Solomon's palace to test him with hard questions? What was her motivation? And why did she bring a very large caravan?

2. What do you think would have happened if the queen had been disappointed by Solomon?

3. What is the significance of the gifts the queen gave Solomon? Why did she give them? What is the significance of the statement, "King Solomon gave the queen of Sheba all she desired and asked for, besides what he had given her out of his royal bounty" (verse 13)?

_____

_____

_____

_____

_____

_____

4. How would you describe the relationship between the two rulers? No further information about the queen of Sheba is given in Scripture, except for another account of her in almost exactly the same words recorded in 2 Chronicles 9:1–12. What would you speculate happened after the queen went home? Who influenced whom after their encounter?

_____

_____

_____

_____

_____

_____

_____

## ③ Relational Rules from the Apostle Paul

### Romans 12:9–21

*⁹ Love must be sincere. Hate what is evil; cling to what is good. ¹⁰ Be devoted to one another in love. Honor one another above yourselves. ¹¹ Never be lacking in zeal, but keep your spiritual fervor, serving the Lord. ¹² Be joyful in hope, patient in affliction, faithful in prayer. ¹³ Share with the Lord's people who are in need. Practice hospitality.*

*14 Bless those who persecute you; bless and do not curse. 15 Rejoice with those who rejoice; mourn with those who mourn. 16 Live in harmony with one another. Do not be proud, but be willing to associate with people of low position. Do not be conceited.*

*17 Do not repay anyone evil for evil. Be careful to do what is right in the eyes of everyone. 18 If it is possible, as far as it depends on you, live at peace with everyone. 19 Do not take revenge, my dear friends, but leave room for God's wrath, for it is written: "It is mine to avenge; I will repay," says the Lord. 20 On the contrary:*

> *"If your enemy is hungry, feed him;*
> *if he is thirsty, give him something to drink.*
> *In doing this, you will heap burning coals on his head."*

*21 Do not be overcome by evil, but overcome evil with good.*

## Study Questions

1. In your own words, how would you summarize how Paul says believers should treat one another? Do you find his advice difficult or easy to follow? Why?

 

 

2. How easy or difficult do you find it to follow Paul's instruction concerning how to treat people who oppose you or who do evil?

 

 

3. How is it possible to "do what is right in the eyes of everyone" (verse 17)? What makes it difficult?

_____

_____

_____

_____

_____

4. How does Paul's advice apply to leadership?

_____

_____

_____

_____

_____

_____

# LEADERSHIP INSIGHT AND REFLECTION

How did the motives of Isaac, Rebekah, Jacob, Esau, the queen of Sheba, Solomon, and Paul impact their relationships?

_____

_____

_____

_____

_____

_____

_____

_____

What role did trust play in the relationships within Isaac's family? Did it increase or decrease? What was the outcome on the family?

_____

_____

_____

_____

_____

_____

_____

_____

What role did trust play in the relationship between King Solomon and the queen of Sheba? Did it increase or decrease? What was the outcome for them?

_____

_____

_____

_____

_____

How can a leader take the advice of Paul, which is to honor one another above ourselves, and still lead effectively?

_____

_____

_____

_____

_____

_____

_____

# TAKING ACTION

Take some time to reflect on how you treat the people you lead, people you follow, people you work with, and people in your family. Where do you need to improve? Are your motives pure? Are you trustworthy? Are you doing your best to honor others? Where is God challenging you to grow and learn?

_____

_____

_____

_____

_____

_____

_____

_____

_____

_____

_____

What action can you take immediately to right a wrong you've done in the past? Are you willing to commit to do it?

_____

_____

_____

_____

_____

_____

_____

_____

_____

_____

_____

_____

_____

**What ongoing action can you take to become better at building relationships, not only in your leadership, but in every area of your life?**

_____

_____

_____

_____

_____

_____

_____

_____

_____

_____

_____

_____

_____

# GROUP DISCUSSION QUESTIONS

1. If you were in Esau's place and had been talked out of your birthright (see Genesis 25:29–34) and tricked out of your blessing by Jacob, how do you think you would have reacted?

2. What words best describe Isaac's family? How does his family compare to yours? What words would you use to describe your family of origin?

3. Do you think the queen of Sheba and King Solomon met as equals? What about after they got to know each other? What, if anything, changed, and why?

4. When you interact with other people, what determines how the relationship unfolds? How do you know who has greater influence on whom? Does your influence change in different environments?

5. Who do you know who does a good job of living by the standards Paul describes in Romans 12? What is the key to that person's ability?

6. What was your greatest takeaway about relationships from this lesson?

7. What action do you believe God is asking you to take as a result? When and how will you do it?

LESSON 16

# RESPONSIBILITY

## If You Won't Carry the Ball,
## You Can't Lead the Team

### THE QUALITY DEFINED

People who embrace responsibility are known for getting things done. They pursue their goals wholeheartedly and never quit. They are the running backs who fight for every yard on the football field and often come through with a touchdown when the game is on the line. Because they demonstrate that they're willing and able to "carry the ball," even in high-pressure situations, their team-mates trust them and work with them for the win. This gives these individuals the credibility to lead.

Responsible leaders begin by taking ownership of their own roles and tasks. Even when they report to someone else, they hold themselves accountable first. They have very high standards, which means they never settle for mediocrity. Instead, they make excellence their objective. Then, as they pursue their goals, they do so with tenacity. They don't give up, and they do everything in their power to finish what they start.

When responsible leaders fail, or make a mistake or bad decision, they readily admit it and apologize. Then they examine what they did wrong, learn from their mistakes, and move forward. They don't make excuses or blame others.

Good leaders never embrace a victim mentality. They recognize that who and where they are is their responsibility—not that of their parents, their spouse, their children, society, the government, their boss, or their coworkers. They face whatever life throws at them and give it their best, knowing that they will only get an opportunity to lead the team if they've proven that they can carry the ball.

# CASE STUDIES

Read these case studies from the Bible and answer the study questions that follow.

## 1 David Owns Up

### 1 Chronicles 21:1–30

*1 Satan rose up against Israel and incited David to take a census of Israel.*
*2 So David said to Joab and the commanders of the troops, "Go and count the Israelites from Beersheba to Dan. Then report back to me so that I may know how many there are."*

*3 But Joab replied, "May the LORD multiply his troops a hundred times over. My lord the king, are they not all my lord's subjects? Why does my lord want to do this? Why should he bring guilt on Israel?"*

*4 The king's word, however, overruled Joab; so Joab left and went throughout Israel and then came back to Jerusalem. 5 Joab reported the number of the fighting men to David: In all Israel there were one million one hundred thousand men who could handle a sword, including four hundred and seventy thousand in Judah.*

*6 But Joab did not include Levi and Benjamin in the numbering, because the king's command was repulsive to him. 7 This command was also evil in the sight of God; so he punished Israel.*

*8 Then David said to God, "I have sinned greatly by doing this. Now, I beg you, take away the guilt of your servant. I have done a very foolish thing."*

*9 The LORD said to Gad, David's seer, 10 "Go and tell David, 'This is what the LORD says: I am giving you three options. Choose one of them for me to carry out against you.'"*

*11 So Gad went to David and said to him, "This is what the LORD says: 'Take your choice: 12 three years of famine, three months of being swept away before your enemies, with their swords overtaking you, or three days of the sword of the LORD—days of plague in the land, with the angel of the LORD ravaging every part of Israel.' Now then, decide how I should answer the one who sent me."*

*13 David said to Gad, "I am in deep distress. Let me fall into the hands of the LORD, for his mercy is very great; but do not let me fall into human hands."*

*14 So the LORD sent a plague on Israel, and seventy thousand men of Israel fell dead. 15 And God sent an angel to destroy Jerusalem. But as the angel was doing so, the LORD saw it and relented concerning the disaster and said to the angel who was destroying the people, "Enough! Withdraw your hand." The angel of the LORD was then standing at the threshing floor of Araunah the Jebusite.*

*16 David looked up and saw the angel of the LORD standing between heaven and earth, with a drawn sword in his hand extended over Jerusalem. Then David and the elders, clothed in sackcloth, fell facedown.*

*17 David said to God, "Was it not I who ordered the fighting men to be counted? I, the shepherd, have sinned and done wrong. These are but sheep. What have they done? LORD my God, let your hand fall on me and my family, but do not let this plague remain on your people."*

*18 Then the angel of the LORD ordered Gad to tell David to go up and build an altar to the LORD on the threshing floor of Araunah the Jebusite. 19 So David went up in obedience to the word that Gad had spoken in the name of the LORD.*

*20 While Araunah was threshing wheat, he turned and saw the angel; his four sons who were with him hid themselves. 21 Then David approached, and when Araunah looked and saw him, he left the threshing floor and bowed down before David with his face to the ground.*

*22 David said to him, "Let me have the site of your threshing floor so I can build an altar to the LORD, that the plague on the people may be stopped. Sell it to me at the full price."*

*23 Araunah said to David, "Take it! Let my lord the king do whatever pleases him. Look, I will give the oxen for the burnt offerings, the threshing sledges for the wood, and the wheat for the grain offering. I will give all this."*

*24 But King David replied to Araunah, "No, I insist on paying the full price. I will not take for the LORD what is yours, or sacrifice a burnt offering that costs me nothing."*

*25 So David paid Araunah six hundred shekels of gold for the site. 26 David built an altar to the LORD there and sacrificed burnt offerings and fellowship offerings. He called on the LORD, and the LORD answered him with fire from heaven on the altar of burnt offering.*

*27 Then the LORD spoke to the angel, and he put his sword back into its sheath. 28 At that time, when David saw that the LORD had answered him on the threshing floor of Araunah the Jebusite, he offered sacrifices there. 29 The tabernacle of the LORD, which Moses had made in the wilderness, and the altar of burnt offering were at that time on the high place at Gibeon. 30 But David could not go before it to inquire of God, because he was afraid of the sword of the angel of the LORD.*

## 1 Chronicles 22:1

*1 Then David said, "The house of the LORD God is to be here, and also the altar of burnt offering for Israel."*

## Study Questions

1. Why would David ask for a census of the fighting men in Israel? Why do you think God considered that a sin?

2. How did David take responsibility for his wrongdoing? List each of the things he did.

_____

_____

_____

_____

_____

_____

3. What do David's responsible choices say about him as a person? What do they say about him as a leader?

_____

_____

_____

_____

_____

_____

4. What is your reaction to David's saying he wanted to be put in God's hands when Gad told him to choose his punishment? What do you think you would have chosen? Why?

_____

_____

_____

_____

_____

_____

## ❷ Jonah Repents and Gets a Second Chance

### Jonah 1:1–17

¹ The word of the LORD came to Jonah son of Amittai: ² "Go to the great city of Nineveh and preach against it, because its wickedness has come up before me."

³ But Jonah ran away from the LORD and headed for Tarshish. He went down to Joppa, where he found a ship bound for that port. After paying the fare, he went aboard and sailed for Tarshish to flee from the LORD.

⁴ Then the LORD sent a great wind on the sea, and such a violent storm arose that the ship threatened to break up. ⁵ All the sailors were afraid and each cried out to his own god. And they threw the cargo into the sea to lighten the ship.

But Jonah had gone below deck, where he lay down and fell into a deep sleep. ⁶ The captain went to him and said, "How can you sleep? Get up and call on your god! Maybe he will take notice of us so that we will not perish."

⁷ Then the sailors said to each other, "Come, let us cast lots to find out who is responsible for this calamity." They cast lots and the lot fell on Jonah. ⁸ So they asked him, "Tell us, who is responsible for making all this trouble for us? What kind of work do you do? Where do you come from? What is your country? From what people are you?"

⁹ He answered, "I am a Hebrew and I worship the LORD, the God of heaven, who made the sea and the dry land."

¹⁰ This terrified them and they asked, "What have you done?" (They knew he was running away from the LORD, because he had already told them so.)

¹¹ The sea was getting rougher and rougher. So they asked him, "What should we do to you to make the sea calm down for us?"

¹² "Pick me up and throw me into the sea," he replied, "and it will become calm. I know that it is my fault that this great storm has come upon you."

¹³ Instead, the men did their best to row back to land. But they could not, for the sea grew even wilder than before. ¹⁴ Then they cried out to the LORD, "Please, LORD, do not let us die for taking this man's life. Do not hold

us accountable for killing an innocent man, for you, LORD, have done as you pleased." [15] Then they took Jonah and threw him overboard, and the raging sea grew calm. [16] At this the men greatly feared the LORD, and they offered a sacrifice to the LORD and made vows to him.

[17] Now the LORD provided a huge fish to swallow Jonah, and Jonah was in the belly of the fish three days and three nights.

## Jonah 2:1–10

[1] From inside the fish Jonah prayed to the LORD his God. [2] He said:

> "In my distress I called to the LORD,
>     and he answered me.
> From deep in the realm of the dead I called for help,
>     and you listened to my cry.
> [3] You hurled me into the depths,
>     into the very heart of the seas,
>     and the currents swirled about me;
> all your waves and breakers
>     swept over me.
> [4] I said, 'I have been banished
>     from your sight;
> yet I will look again
>     toward your holy temple.'
> [5] The engulfing waters threatened me,
>     the deep surrounded me;
>     seaweed was wrapped around my head.
> [6] To the roots of the mountains I sank down;
>     the earth beneath barred me in forever.
> But you, LORD my God,
>     brought my life up from the pit.
>
> [7] "When my life was ebbing away,
>     I remembered you, LORD,

and my prayer rose to you,
     to your holy temple.

8 "Those who cling to worthless idols
     turn away from God's love for them.
9 But I, with shouts of grateful praise,
     will sacrifice to you.
What I have vowed I will make good.
     I will say, 'Salvation comes from the LORD.'"

10 And the LORD commanded the fish, and it vomited Jonah onto dry land.

## Jonah 3:1–10

1 Then the word of the LORD came to Jonah a second time: 2 "Go to the great city of Nineveh and proclaim to it the message I give you."

3 Jonah obeyed the word of the LORD and went to Nineveh. Now Nineveh was a very large city; it took three days to go through it. 4 Jonah began by going a day's journey into the city, proclaiming, "Forty more days and Nineveh will be overthrown." 5 The Ninevites believed God. A fast was proclaimed, and all of them, from the greatest to the least, put on sackcloth.

6 When Jonah's warning reached the king of Nineveh, he rose from his throne, took off his royal robes, covered himself with sackcloth and sat down in the dust. 7 This is the proclamation he issued in Nineveh:

"By the decree of the king and his nobles:
     Do not let people or animals, herds or flocks, taste anything; do not let them eat or drink. 8 But let people and animals be covered with sackcloth. Let everyone call urgently on God. Let them give up their evil ways and their violence. 9 Who knows? God may yet relent and with compassion turn from his fierce anger so that we will not perish."

10 When God saw what they did and how they turned from their evil ways, he relented and did not bring on them the destruction he had threatened.

## Study Questions

1. Do you think Jonah believed he truly could run away from God? Or was he simply trying to put himself in a place where it would be impossible for him to obey God? Have you ever done something similar? If so, what did you do and why?

_____

_____

_____

_____

2. What was the indication that Jonah was starting to take responsibility? Did he take further action? If so, what was it?

_____

_____

_____

_____

3. Why do you think God gave Jonah a second chance? Why didn't God just pick someone else to go to Nineveh? What does that say about God?

_____

_____

_____

_____

_____

## ❸ Pilate Washes His Hands

### Matthew 27:11–26

[11] *Meanwhile Jesus stood before the governor, and the governor asked him, "Are you the king of the Jews?"*

*"You have said so," Jesus replied.*

[12] *When he was accused by the chief priests and the elders, he gave no answer.* [13] *Then Pilate asked him, "Don't you hear the testimony they are bringing against you?"* [14] *But Jesus made no reply, not even to a single charge—to the great amazement of the governor.*

[15] *Now it was the governor's custom at the festival to release a prisoner chosen by the crowd.* [16] *At that time they had a well-known prisoner whose name was Jesus Barabbas.* [17] *So when the crowd had gathered, Pilate asked them, "Which one do you want me to release to you: Jesus Barabbas, or Jesus who is called the Messiah?"* [18] *For he knew it was out of self-interest that they had handed Jesus over to him.*

[19] *While Pilate was sitting on the judge's seat, his wife sent him this message: "Don't have anything to do with that innocent man, for I have suffered a great deal today in a dream because of him."*

[20] *But the chief priests and the elders persuaded the crowd to ask for Barabbas and to have Jesus executed.*

[21] *"Which of the two do you want me to release to you?" asked the governor.*

*"Barabbas," they answered.*

[22] *"What shall I do, then, with Jesus who is called the Messiah?" Pilate asked. They all answered, "Crucify him!"*

[23] *"Why? What crime has he committed?" asked Pilate.*

*But they shouted all the louder, "Crucify him!"*

[24] *When Pilate saw that he was getting nowhere, but that instead an uproar was starting, he took water and washed his hands in front of the crowd. "I am innocent of this man's blood," he said. "It is your responsibility!"*

[25] *All the people answered, "His blood is on us and on our children!"*

[26] *Then he released Barabbas to them. But he had Jesus flogged, and handed him over to be crucified.*

## Study Questions

1. Think about all the people involved in this passage. What levels of responsibility did each *claim* and what responsibility did they actually *take*?

   Jesus Claimed: _____

   Jesus Took: _____

   Pilate Claimed: _____

   Pilate Took: _____

   Pilate's Wife Claimed: _____

   Pilate's Wife Took: _____

   The Chief Priest and Elders Claimed: _____

   The Chief Priest and Elders Took: _____

   The People Claimed: _____

   The People Took: _____

2. What was the motivation for each of them for what they did?

   Jesus: _____

   Pilate: _____

   Pilate's Wife: _____

   Chief Priest and Elders: _____

   The People: _____

3. Would the actions of any of them have changed if they had understood what Jesus was doing and why? Explain your answer.

   _____

   _____

   _____

   _____

   _____

   _____

# LEADERSHIP INSIGHT AND REFLECTION

Once a leader has made a decision, how difficult do you think it is for him or her to reverse course on it, even if it was wrong? What caused David to change course? What caused Jonah to do so? Why didn't Pilate reverse his decision?

_____

_____

_____

_____

_____

_____

How do you believe people usually accept responsibility? Does it come all at once? Is it typically progressively accepted? Describe the process.

_____

_____

_____

_____

_____

_____

In which areas of your life do you find it most challenging to take responsibility? In which areas do you find it easier? What motivation usually prompts you to be responsible in the areas where you are successful?

_____

_____

_____

_____

_____

_____

_____

# TAKING ACTION

Where in your life do you need to take greater responsibility? How can you harness the motivation that usually helps you?

_____

_____

_____

_____

_____

How will taking responsibility in that area help you to become a better leader?

_____

_____

_____

_____

What first step will you take immediately?

_____

_____

_____

_____

_____

_____

_____

# GROUP DISCUSSION QUESTIONS

1. When David stated he wanted to conduct a census, Joab, who was the commander of his army, warned against it, yet David ordered the census anyway. Have you ever been in a position similar to Joab's where your good advice wasn't accepted by a leader? What happened?

2. After making his bad decision, David took responsibility for it. How does that impact your opinion of him?

3. Were you surprised when Jonah advised the sailors to throw him overboard? Were you surprised when the sailors at first refused? What do their actions say about their sense of responsibility?

4. Taking into account the actions of the chief priest and elders, Pilate, Jesus, and the crowd, who would you say was responsible for Jesus' death?

5. Why did Pilate wash his hands before the crowd? What did his actions actually accomplish?

6. How would you rate your innate level of responsibility on a scale from 1 (irresponsible) to 10 (hyper-responsible)? How is it helping or hurting your leadership ability?

7. What specific action do you believe God is asking you to take in your leadership growth as a result of this lesson? When and how will you do it?

# SECURITY

## Competence Never Compensates
## for Insecurity

## THE QUALITY DEFINED

The successful twentieth century industrialist and philanthropist Andrew Carnegie once said, "No one will make a great leader who wants to do it all himself or get all the credit for doing it." He was right. It's not enough for a leader to be a competent worker; effective leadership means making the transition from doer to leader, and that requires a level of personal security to succeed.

Secure leaders embrace their role. They understand that when they choose to lead, they also choose to define their own success based on the team's success. They see more value in collaboration than in competition. As a result, they don't feel threatened by the accomplishments of their people, and they gladly share power and credit with them.

Secure leaders believe in themselves and their people. Because they're confident in their own strengths and realistic about their weaknesses, they are able to appreciate the talents of team members and to accept their flaws. And they consistently communicate their belief in their people, celebrating and encouraging their accomplishments.

Secure leaders also give more credit than they take and accept more blame than they give. While leaders with a deep internal need for validation or acknowledgement from others have a very hard time offering those things to others, secure leaders want to help their followers shine. And when things go wrong, the buck stops with them. They own it on behalf of the team.

A leadership position is an amplifier of personal flaws. Leaders who are insecure are incapable of offering security to their followers, because they cannot give what they do not have. They tend to feel threatened by the success of others, so they hoard power or undermine their people, making it difficult for team members to achieve their goals. And if their people somehow manage to succeed in spite of them, these leaders claim all the credit. When followers are undermined and receive no recognition, they become discouraged and eventually stop performing to their full potential. And when that happens, the entire organization suffers.

# CASE STUDIES

Read these case studies from the Bible and answer the study questions that follow.

## ❶ Moses and His Siblings

### Numbers 12:1–15

*1 Miriam and Aaron began to talk against Moses because of his Cushite wife, for he had married a Cushite. 2 "Has the LORD spoken only through Moses?" they asked. "Hasn't he also spoken through us?" And the LORD heard this.*

*3 (Now Moses was a very humble man, more humble than anyone else on the face of the earth.)*

*4 At once the LORD said to Moses, Aaron and Miriam, "Come out to the tent of meeting, all three of you." So the three of them went out. 5 Then the LORD came down in a pillar of cloud; he stood at the entrance to the tent and summoned Aaron and Miriam. When the two of them stepped forward, 6 he said, "Listen to my words:*

*"When there is a prophet among you,*
*I, the LORD, reveal myself to them in visions,*
*I speak to them in dreams.*

*⁷ But this is not true of my servant Moses;*
*he is faithful in all my house.*
*⁸ With him I speak face to face,*
*clearly and not in riddles;*
*he sees the form of the LORD.*
*Why then were you not afraid*
*to speak against my servant Moses?"*

*⁹ The anger of the LORD burned against them, and he left them.*
*¹⁰ When the cloud lifted from above the tent, Miriam's skin was leprous—it became as white as snow. Aaron turned toward her and saw that she had a defiling skin disease, ¹¹ and he said to Moses, "Please, my lord, I ask you not to hold against us the sin we have so foolishly committed. ¹² Do not let her be like a stillborn infant coming from its mother's womb with its flesh half eaten away."*

*¹³ So Moses cried out to the LORD, "Please, God, heal her!"*

*¹⁴ The LORD replied to Moses, "If her father had spit in her face, would she not have been in disgrace for seven days? Confine her outside the camp for seven days; after that she can be brought back." ¹⁵ So Miriam was confined outside the camp for seven days, and the people did not move on till she was brought back.*

## Study Questions

1. Why did Miriam, the older sister of Moses (see Exodus 2:4,7) and also a prophet (see Exodus 15:20), speak out against Moses along with her brother, Aaron? How much do you think it really had to do with his Cushite wife?

   _____

   _____

   _____

   _____

   _____

   _____

   _____

2. If you had been in Moses' place and your critical siblings had been punished by God, how would you have felt? Justified? Protective? Empathetic? Explain.

_____

_____

_____

_____

_____

_____

_____

3. What does it say about Moses that he immediately begged God to heal his sister?

_____

_____

_____

_____

_____

_____

_____

4. The passage says Moses was "more humble than anyone else on the face of the earth" (verse 3), yet his actions were those of a completely secure leader. How do you reconcile these two facets of his personality?

_____

_____

_____

_____

_____

_____

_____

_____

## ❷ Saul Fears David's Success

### 1 Samuel 18:1–16

*¹ After David had finished talking with Saul, Jonathan became one in spirit with David, and he loved him as himself. ² From that day Saul kept David with him and did not let him return home to his family. ³ And Jonathan made a covenant with David because he loved him as himself. ⁴ Jonathan took off the robe he was wearing and gave it to David, along with his tunic, and even his sword, his bow and his belt.*

*⁵ Whatever mission Saul sent him on, David was so successful that Saul gave him a high rank in the army. This pleased all the troops, and Saul's officers as well.*

*⁶ When the men were returning home after David had killed the Philistine, the women came out from all the towns of Israel to meet King Saul with singing and dancing, with joyful songs and with timbrels and lyres. ⁷ As they danced, they sang:*

> *"Saul has slain his thousands,*
> *and David his tens of thousands."*

*⁸ Saul was very angry; this refrain displeased him greatly. "They have credited David with tens of thousands," he thought, "but me with only thousands. What more can he get but the kingdom?" ⁹ And from that time on Saul kept a close eye on David.*

*¹⁰ The next day an evil spirit from God came forcefully on Saul. He was prophesying in his house, while David was playing the lyre, as he usually did. Saul had a spear in his hand ¹¹ and he hurled it, saying to himself, "I'll pin David to the wall." But David eluded him twice.*

*¹² Saul was afraid of David, because the Lord was with David but had departed from Saul. ¹³ So he sent David away from him and gave him command over a thousand men, and David led the troops in their campaigns. ¹⁴ In everything he did he had great success, because the Lord was with him. ¹⁵ When Saul saw how successful he was, he was afraid of him. ¹⁶ But all Israel and Judah loved David, because he led them in their campaigns.*

## Study Questions

1. What flaw in Saul made him react so negatively to David?

2. Do you think David's acceptance by Jonathan, Saul's heir, should have made Saul feel more or less threatened by David? Explain your thinking.

3. What might have happened if Saul had celebrated David's victories and rewarded him publicly instead of trying to kill him?

4. What can leaders do to keep leading effectively and making their organization successful when someone they lead is talented, favored by God, successful, and receiving recognition?

## 3 Nathan Rebukes a King

### 2 Samuel 12:1–19

*[1] The Lord sent Nathan to David. When he came to him, he said, "There were two men in a certain town, one rich and the other poor. [2] The rich man had a very large number of sheep and cattle, [3] but the poor man had nothing except one little ewe lamb he had bought. He raised it, and it grew up with him and his children. It shared his food, drank from his cup and even slept in his arms. It was like a daughter to him.*

*[4] "Now a traveler came to the rich man, but the rich man refrained from taking one of his own sheep or cattle to prepare a meal for the traveler who had come to him. Instead, he took the ewe lamb that belonged to the poor man and prepared it for the one who had come to him."*

*[5] David burned with anger against the man and said to Nathan, "As surely as the Lord lives, the man who did this must die! [6] He must pay for that lamb four times over, because he did such a thing and had no pity."*

*[7] Then Nathan said to David, "You are the man! This is what the Lord, the God of Israel, says: 'I anointed you king over Israel, and I delivered you from the hand of Saul. [8] I gave your master's house to you, and your master's wives into your arms. I gave you all Israel and Judah. And if all this had been too little, I would have given you even more. [9] Why did you despise the word of the Lord by doing what is evil in his eyes? You struck down Uriah the Hittite with the sword and took his wife to be your own. You killed him with the sword of the Ammonites. [10] Now, therefore, the sword will never depart from your house, because you despised me and took the wife of Uriah the Hittite to be your own.'*

*[11] "This is what the Lord says: 'Out of your own household I am going to bring calamity on you. Before your very eyes I will take your wives and give them to one who is close to you, and he will sleep with your wives in broad daylight. [12] You did it in secret, but I will do this thing in broad daylight before all Israel.'"*

*[13] Then David said to Nathan, "I have sinned against the Lord."*

*Nathan replied, "The Lord has taken away your sin. You are not going to die. [14] But because by doing this you have shown utter contempt for the Lord, the son born to you will die."*

<sup>15</sup> *After Nathan had gone home, the L*ORD *struck the child that Uriah's wife had borne to David, and he became ill.* <sup>16</sup> *David pleaded with God for the child. He fasted and spent the nights lying in sackcloth on the ground.* <sup>17</sup> *The elders of his household stood beside him to get him up from the ground, but he refused, and he would not eat any food with them.*

<sup>18</sup> *On the seventh day the child died. David's attendants were afraid to tell him that the child was dead, for they thought, "While the child was still living, he wouldn't listen to us when we spoke to him. How can we now tell him the child is dead? He may do something desperate."*

<sup>19</sup> *David noticed that his attendants were whispering among themselves, and he realized the child was dead. "Is the child dead?" he asked.*

*"Yes," they replied, "he is dead."*

## Study Questions

1. Why did Nathan confront David? Couldn't he have kept silent and waited for God to punish the king?

_____

_____

_____

_____

_____

_____

2. How much do you think David's security in his own leadership factored into Nathan's willingness to confront and rebuke him?

_____

_____

_____

_____

_____

_____

_____

3. If you had been confronted for your wrongdoing by a subordinate like Nathan, how do you think you would have reacted? How do you respond when people on your team disagree with you or challenge you?

_____

_____

_____

_____

_____

_____

_____

# LEADERSHIP INSIGHT AND REFLECTION

Which leaders from these passages can you identify with: Miriam, Aaron, Moses, Saul, David, Jonathan, or Nathan? What makes you relate to them?

_____

_____

_____

_____

_____

_____

What are the qualities of a secure leader, based on what you read in these passages as well as on your own experience and observations? Describe them.

_____

_____

_____

_____

_____

_____

_____

Which of those qualities do you possess, and which do you lack?

_____

_____

_____

_____

_____

_____

_____

# TAKING ACTION

Becoming secure as a leader often takes deep work within a person and requires the assistance of God. Take some time to pray, asking God for his help. Then answer these questions.

In what situations do you act insecurely?

_____

_____

_____

_____

_____

_____

What might be some of the causes of your insecurity? (Ask God to help you with this, and then write whatever comes to mind.)

_____

_____

_____

_____

_____

_____

_____

_____

_____

How would your leadership improve if you became better at giving others credit, taking blame yourself when the team fails, and celebrating when people around you are successful?

_____

_____

_____

_____

_____

_____

How might God be asking you to change? How do you want God to help you?

_____

_____

_____

_____

_____

_____

_____

# GROUP DISCUSSION QUESTIONS

1. How do you think Moses felt when the two people closest to him started to complain about him?

2. How do you typically handle criticism when you receive it? What determines how you respond?

3. Have you ever been in a position where a sibling, coworker, or colleague constantly received recognition and you felt overshadowed or overlooked? How did you react?

4. Saul promoted David when he was successful, yet he also tried to kill him. Why was Saul so inconsistent? What kind of environment does that kind of leadership create?

5. David became angry when Nathan told him the story of the ewe lamb. When Nathan said, "You are the man" (2 Samuel 12:7), David could have directed his anger at Nathan and become defensive. Instead, he was repentant. What qualities in David made that possible?

6. What was your greatest takeaway about yourself related to security from this lesson?

7. How do you need to change to become more secure as a leader? What will you do, and when will you do it?

# SELF-DISCIPLINE

## The First Person You Lead Is You

### THE QUALITY DEFINED

The hardest person to lead is always yourself. But leaders *must* lead themselves first before they can effectively influence anyone else. One reason for this is that it's extremely challenging to follow an undisciplined leader. Followers benefit from clear direction and planning; otherwise, they feel like they're at the mercy of the leader's whims. And this makes them less trusting of their leader. In addition, self-discipline itself is not easy to learn or practice. Followers need to see it modeled by their leader over time in order to embrace and sustain it themselves.

What is self-discipline in a leader? It is regular, consistent, ongoing practice of activities that produce a long-term benefit for the leader and the team. It is a lifestyle or habit, not a one-time promise or event. Leaders with self-discipline know what is important and why. They have determined their highest priorities. They also know and can explain their reasons for them.

They also commit to goals. They have "drawn a line in the sand" by declaring their intentions either aloud or in writing before others. And when discipline becomes difficult, such as when they're distracted or discouraged, they remind themselves of the benefits of staying the course.

One of the ways leaders maintain their self-discipline is by creating routines and systems for themselves. And they hold themselves accountable for sticking to them. That way important tasks are less likely to be forgotten or displaced by other activities.

Self-discipline is the key to sustained success in leadership. Only leaders who lead themselves consistently through a lifestyle of self-discipline can achieve their long-term goals in the long run. This empowers their followers to reach their potential in the long run, too.

# CASE STUDIES

Read these case studies from the Bible and answer the study questions that follow.

## 1 The Psalmist Prays for Self-Discipline

### Psalm 119:1–16

1 *Blessed are those whose ways are blameless,*
*who walk according to the law of the LORD.*
2 *Blessed are those who keep his statutes*
*and seek him with all their heart—*
3 *they do no wrong*
*but follow his ways.*
4 *You have laid down precepts*
*that are to be fully obeyed.*
5 *Oh, that my ways were steadfast*
*in obeying your decrees!*
6 *Then I would not be put to shame*
*when I consider all your commands.*
7 *I will praise you with an upright heart*
*as I learn your righteous laws.*
8 *I will obey your decrees;*
*do not utterly forsake me.*

*⁹ How can a young person stay on the path of purity?*

*By living according to your word.*

*¹⁰ I seek you with all my heart;*

*do not let me stray from your commands.*

*¹¹ I have hidden your word in my heart*

*that I might not sin against you.*

*¹² Praise be to you, LORD;*

*teach me your decrees.*

*¹³ With my lips I recount*

*all the laws that come from your mouth.*

*¹⁴ I rejoice in following your statutes*

*as one rejoices in great riches.*

*¹⁵ I meditate on your precepts*

*and consider your ways.*

*¹⁶ I delight in your decrees;*

*I will not neglect your word.*

## Study Questions

1. Why do you think the psalmist wrote this psalm? What might have prompted it?

_____

_____

_____

_____

2. What are the benefits of self-discipline? How does the psalmist describe them?

_____

_____

_____

_____

_____

_____

3. How can one go about practicing self-discipline? Upon what is it based?

_____

_____

_____

_____

_____

_____

_____

## 2 Jesus Prepares to Start His Ministry

### Luke 4:1–21

[1] *Jesus, full of the Holy Spirit, left the Jordan and was led by the Spirit into the wilderness,* [2] *where for forty days he was tempted by the devil. He ate nothing during those days, and at the end of them he was hungry.*

[3] *The devil said to him, "If you are the Son of God, tell this stone to become bread."*

[4] *Jesus answered, "It is written: 'Man shall not live on bread alone.'"*

[5] *The devil led him up to a high place and showed him in an instant all the kingdoms of the world.* [6] *And he said to him, "I will give you all their authority and splendor; it has been given to me, and I can give it to anyone I want to.* [7] *If you worship me, it will all be yours."*

[8] *Jesus answered, "It is written: 'Worship the Lord your God and serve him only.'"*

[9] *The devil led him to Jerusalem and had him stand on the highest point of the temple. "If you are the Son of God," he said, "throw yourself down from here.* [10] *For it is written:*

> *"'He will command his angels concerning you*
>     *to guard you carefully;*
> [11] *they will lift you up in their hands,*
>     *so that you will not strike your foot against a stone.'"*

<sup>12</sup> *Jesus answered, "It is said: 'Do not put the Lord your God to the test.'"*
<sup>13</sup> *When the devil had finished all this tempting, he left him until an opportune time.*

<sup>14</sup> *Jesus returned to Galilee in the power of the Spirit, and news about him spread through the whole countryside.* <sup>15</sup> *He was teaching in their synagogues, and everyone praised him.*

<sup>16</sup> *He went to Nazareth, where he had been brought up, and on the Sabbath day he went into the synagogue, as was his custom. He stood up to read,* <sup>17</sup> *and the scroll of the prophet Isaiah was handed to him. Unrolling it, he found the place where it is written:*

<sup>18</sup> *"The Spirit of the Lord is on me,*
*because he has anointed me*
*to proclaim good news to the poor.*
*He has sent me to proclaim freedom for the prisoners*
*and recovery of sight for the blind,*
*to set the oppressed free,*
<sup>19</sup> *to proclaim the year of the Lord's favor."*

<sup>20</sup> *Then he rolled up the scroll, gave it back to the attendant and sat down. The eyes of everyone in the synagogue were fastened on him.* <sup>21</sup> *He began by saying to them, "Today this scripture is fulfilled in your hearing."*

## Study Questions

1. Why do you think the Holy Spirit led Jesus into the wilderness where he would be tempted?

2. How did Jesus deal with temptation? What was the key to his ability to resist it?

_____

_____

_____

3. What kinds of temptations did Jesus face? What kinds of temptations do most leaders face?

_____

_____

_____

_____

_____

4. When Jesus read the Isaiah scroll and stated the scripture was being fulfilled, he started his public ministry. How did his time in the wilderness prepare him for that?

_____

_____

_____

## ❸ Paul's Advice

### 1 Corinthians 9:24–27

*24 Do you not know that in a race all the runners run, but only one gets the prize? Run in such a way as to get the prize. 25 Everyone who competes in the games goes into strict training. They do it to get a crown that will not last, but we do it to get a crown that will last forever. 26 Therefore I do not run like someone running aimlessly; I do not fight like a boxer beating the air. 27 No, I strike a blow to my body and make it my slave so that after I have preached to others, I myself will not be disqualified for the prize.*

## 1 Corinthians 10:1–13, 23–24

*¹ For I do not want you to be ignorant of the fact, brothers and sisters, that our ancestors were all under the cloud and that they all passed through the sea. ² They were all baptized into Moses in the cloud and in the sea. ³ They all ate the same spiritual food ⁴ and drank the same spiritual drink; for they drank from the spiritual rock that accompanied them, and that rock was Christ. ⁵ Nevertheless, God was not pleased with most of them; their bodies were scattered in the wilderness.*

*⁶ Now these things occurred as examples to keep us from setting our hearts on evil things as they did. ⁷ Do not be idolaters, as some of them were; as it is written: "The people sat down to eat and drink and got up to indulge in revelry." ⁸ We should not commit sexual immorality, as some of them did—and in one day twenty-three thousand of them died. ⁹ We should not test Christ, as some of them did—and were killed by snakes. ¹⁰ And do not grumble, as some of them did—and were killed by the destroying angel.*

*¹¹ These things happened to them as examples and were written down as warnings for us, on whom the culmination of the ages has come. ¹² So, if you think you are standing firm, be careful that you don't fall! ¹³ No temptation has overtaken you except what is common to mankind. And God is faithful; he will not let you be tempted beyond what you can bear. But when you are tempted, he will also provide a way out so that you can endure it. . . .*

*²³ "I have the right to do anything," you say—but not everything is beneficial. "I have the right to do anything"—but not everything is constructive. ²⁴ No one should seek their own good, but the good of others.*

## Study Questions

1. How does Paul describe the way we should train in self-discipline? How well do you relate to his analogy? Explain.

   _____

   _____

   _____

   _____

2. Why do you think Paul describes what happened to the children of Israel during the Exodus in this teaching on how we should conduct ourselves?

_____

_____

_____

_____

_____

_____

_____

3. What is your reaction to Paul's statement that God won't allow people to be tempted beyond what they can bear? Does that encourage you? Make you feel guilty for past lapses in self-discipline? Both? Explain.

_____

_____

_____

_____

_____

_____

_____

_____

_____

4. How can you use the knowledge of Paul's statement to strengthen your self-discipline going forward?

_____

_____

_____

_____

_____

_____

_____

5. In Romans, Paul states that followers of Christ are not under the law, but under grace (see 6:15–16). That idea is echoed here, but Paul also says that even though we have the right to do anything, everything we do is not constructive or beneficial. What are some examples of that? And how does self-discipline come into play in what we choose to do?

_____

_____

_____

_____

_____

_____

# LEADERSHIP INSIGHT AND REFLECTION

How did the approaches to self-discipline of the psalmist, Jesus, and Paul differ? How were they similar?

_____

_____

_____

_____

_____

_____

Based on the passages, what are the guidelines or components that empower someone to practice godly self-discipline?

_____

_____

_____

_____

_____

_____

How successful are you in living out those guidelines every day? Where do you succeed, and where do you struggle?

_____

_____

_____

_____

_____

_____

_____

_____

What goals do you have as a leader that you are currently failing to accomplish because your self-discipline isn't strong enough?

_____

_____

_____

_____

_____

_____

_____

What would change for you, your team, and your organization if you were able to practice better self-discipline and achieve those objectives?

_____

_____

_____

_____

_____

_____

_____

_____

# TAKING ACTION

What one specific concrete step do you need to take to become more self-disciplined and become a better leader?

_____

_____

_____

_____

_____

_____

When is the *soonest* you can take that step? _____

How long will you intentionally sustain it and follow through with it for it to become a positive habit? Twenty-one days? Thirty days? Longer? Write your commitment here.

_____

_____

_____

_____

_____

_____

_____

_____

_____

_____

_____

_____

_____

# Group Discussion Questions

1. Do you agree the hardest person to lead is always yourself? Explain your answer.

2. Which parts of the Psalms passage in this lesson deal with self-leadership?

3. Paul said that when we're tempted, God always provides a way out. How has this been true for you? Where have you been tempted but been able to resist giving in to it?

4. What areas are chronically difficult for you when it comes to temptation? Where has God provided ways out that you've missed in the past? How can you become better at using those ways out?

5. Where did the psalmist, Jesus, and Paul look for the source of their self-discipline? Where should you look for yours?

6. What was your greatest takeaway about self-discipline from this lesson?

7. What action do you believe God is asking you to take to become more self-disciplined? When and how will you follow through with it?

# SERVANTHOOD

## The Right Heart Will Take You a Long Way

## THE QUALITY DEFINED

When you think of servanthood, do you envision it as an activity performed by relatively low-skilled people at the bottom of the organizational chart? If so, you have a wrong impression. Servanthood is not about position, status, or skill. In fact, Jesus made that clear when he taught that the greatest must become the least. The org chart really should be turned upside-down. The higher the leaders, the more they should serve. They surrender their own agenda to that of their followers. This is more than a willingness to put their agenda on hold. It means intentionally choosing to learn about people's needs, to value those needs above their own, and to take concrete action to meet them.

Servanthood should never be motivated by manipulation or self-promotion. Often, servanthood demonstrated by a leader results in a willingness to follow by their people. But that should never be the goal. True servant leaders are motivated by love and unselfishness. They serve their followers because they want what is best for them.

Because servant leaders must put the needs of others first, they first must be secure in themselves. Insecurity is the enemy of servanthood. Leaders who believe they are too important to serve are essentially insecure. After all, how we treat others is really a reflection of how we think about ourselves. Leaders who accept and believe in themselves are the most capable of demonstrating acceptance and belief to others.

To be a servant, a leader should be willing to go first. Just about anyone will serve if compelled to do so. And some will serve in a crisis. But when leaders initiate service to others, they reveal their heart. Servant leaders see the need, seize the opportunity, and serve without expecting anything in return.

Becoming a servant leader is the right thing to do according to God's Word. But it's also the practical thing to do. People don't enjoy following leaders who demand servitude. They willingly follow leaders who seek to serve them. When leaders put others first, followers tend to do likewise. This creates an enjoyable and productive team environment. And all are free to succeed together.

# CASE STUDIES

Read these case studies from the Bible and answer the study questions that follow.

## ❶ David Stands Up for the Men Who Stayed Behind

### 1 Samuel 30:1–31

*1 David and his men reached Ziklag on the third day. Now the Amalekites had raided the Negev and Ziklag. They had attacked Ziklag and burned it, 2 and had taken captive the women and everyone else in it, both young and old. They killed none of them, but carried them off as they went on their way.*

*3 When David and his men reached Ziklag, they found it destroyed by fire and their wives and sons and daughters taken captive. 4 So David and his men wept aloud until they had no strength left to weep. 5 David's two wives had been captured—Ahinoam of Jezreel and Abigail, the widow of Nabal of Carmel. 6 David was greatly distressed because the men were talking of stoning him; each one was bitter in spirit because of his sons and daughters. But David found strength in the LORD his God.*

*7 Then David said to Abiathar the priest, the son of Ahimelek, "Bring me the ephod." Abiathar brought it to him, 8 and David inquired of the LORD, "Shall I pursue this raiding party? Will I overtake them?"*

*"Pursue them," he answered. "You will certainly overtake them and succeed in the rescue."*

*9 David and the six hundred men with him came to the Besor Valley, where some stayed behind. 10 Two hundred of them were too exhausted to cross the valley, but David and the other four hundred continued the pursuit.*

*11 They found an Egyptian in a field and brought him to David. They gave him water to drink and food to eat— 12 part of a cake of pressed figs and two cakes of raisins. He ate and was revived, for he had not eaten any food or drunk any water for three days and three nights.*

*13 David asked him, "Who do you belong to? Where do you come from?"*

*He said, "I am an Egyptian, the slave of an Amalekite. My master abandoned me when I became ill three days ago. 14 We raided the Negev of the Kerethites, some territory belonging to Judah and the Negev of Caleb. And we burned Ziklag."*

*15 David asked him, "Can you lead me down to this raiding party?"*

*He answered, "Swear to me before God that you will not kill me or hand me over to my master, and I will take you down to them."*

*16 He led David down, and there they were, scattered over the countryside, eating, drinking and reveling because of the great amount of plunder they had taken from the land of the Philistines and from Judah. 17 David fought them from dusk until the evening of the next day, and none of them got away, except four hundred young men who rode off on camels and fled. 18 David recovered everything the Amalekites had taken, including his two wives. 19 Nothing was missing: young or old, boy or girl, plunder or anything else they had taken. David brought everything back. 20 He took all the flocks and herds, and his men drove them ahead of the other livestock, saying, "This is David's plunder."*

*21 Then David came to the two hundred men who had been too exhausted to follow him and who were left behind at the Besor Valley. They came out to meet David and the men with him. As David and his men approached, he asked them how they were. 22 But all the evil men and troublemakers among David's followers said, "Because they did not go out with us, we will not share with them the plunder we recovered. However, each man may take his wife and children and go."*

*23 David replied, "No, my brothers, you must not do that with what the LORD has given us. He has protected us and delivered into our hands the raiding party that came against us. 24 Who will listen to what you say? The share of the man who stayed with the supplies is to be the same as that of him who went down to the battle. All will share alike." 25 David made this a statute and ordinance for Israel from that day to this.*

*26 When David reached Ziklag, he sent some of the plunder to the elders of Judah, who were his friends, saying, "Here is a gift for you from the plunder of the LORD's enemies."*

*27 David sent it to those who were in Bethel, Ramoth Negev and Jattir; 28 to those in Aroer, Siphmoth, Eshtemoa 29 and Rakal; to those in the towns of the Jerahmeelites and the Kenites; 30 to those in Hormah, Bor Ashan, Athak 31 and Hebron; and to those in all the other places where he and his men had roamed.*

## Study Questions

1. Do you consider David's decision to share the plunder equally to be fair and just or generous and indulgent? Explain.

   _____

   _____

   _____

   _____

   _____

2. What might have motivated David to make that decision? And why do you think he sent some of the plunder to the elders of Judah?

   _____

   _____

   _____

   _____

3. Why do you think the victorious fighting men declared the additional flocks and herds to be David's plunder? Why didn't David take that to heart and keep everything for himself?

_____

_____

_____

_____

_____

_____

4. How would you describe David's leadership skill and style in this passage? How did he handle the discovery that their families had been taken? How did he handle the battle? How did he handle the dispute between the four hundred men and the two hundred who stayed behind? How did he handle relations with people in the area?

_____

_____

_____

_____

_____

_____

_____

_____

## ② The Samaritan Stops to Help

### Luke 10:25–37

<sup>25</sup> *On one occasion an expert in the law stood up to test Jesus. "Teacher,"*
*he asked, "what must I do to inherit eternal life?"*

*<sup>26</sup> "What is written in the Law?" he replied. "How do you read it?"*

*<sup>27</sup> He answered, "'Love the Lord your God with all your heart and with all*
*your soul and with all your strength and with all your mind'; and, 'Love your*
*neighbor as yourself.'"*

<sup>28</sup> *"You have answered correctly," Jesus replied. "Do this and you will live."*
<sup>29</sup> *But he wanted to justify himself, so he asked Jesus, "And who is my neighbor?"*

<sup>30</sup> *In reply Jesus said: "A man was going down from Jerusalem to Jericho, when he was attacked by robbers. They stripped him of his clothes, beat him and went away, leaving him half dead.* <sup>31</sup> *A priest happened to be going down the same road, and when he saw the man, he passed by on the other side.* <sup>32</sup> *So too, a Levite, when he came to the place and saw him, passed by on the other side.* <sup>33</sup> *But a Samaritan, as he traveled, came where the man was; and when he saw him, he took pity on him.* <sup>34</sup> *He went to him and bandaged his wounds, pouring on oil and wine. Then he put the man on his own donkey, brought him to an inn and took care of him.* <sup>35</sup> *The next day he took out two denarii and gave them to the innkeeper. 'Look after him,' he said, 'and when I return, I will reimburse you for any extra expense you may have.'*

<sup>36</sup> *"Which of these three do you think was a neighbor to the man who fell into the hands of robbers?"*

<sup>37</sup> *The expert in the law replied, "The one who had mercy on him."*
*Jesus told him, "Go and do likewise."*

## Study Questions

1. What was the expert in the law trying to achieve in his dialogue with Jesus? What was the actual outcome?

_____

_____

_____

_____

2. In this parable, why did Jesus choose a priest and a Levite to be the ones who passed the injured man? What point was Jesus trying to make?

_____

_____

_____

3. When Jesus asked the expert in the law who acted like a neighbor, the man responded that it was the person who was merciful. How much does mercy or compassion come into play for servanthood?

_____

_____

_____

_____

4. How can people lead effectively and at the same time also love God and love their neighbor as themselves? How difficult do you find that to be personally?

_____

_____

_____

_____

_____

## ③ Jesus Provides the Ultimate Visual Aid

### John 13:1–17

[1] *It was just before the Passover Festival. Jesus knew that the hour had come for him to leave this world and go to the Father. Having loved his own who were in the world, he loved them to the end.*

[2] *The evening meal was in progress, and the devil had already prompted Judas, the son of Simon Iscariot, to betray Jesus.* [3] *Jesus knew that the Father had put all things under his power, and that he had come from God and was returning to God;* [4] *so he got up from the meal, took off his outer clothing,*

and wrapped a towel around his waist. ⁵ After that, he poured water into a basin and began to wash his disciples' feet, drying them with the towel that was wrapped around him.

⁶ He came to Simon Peter, who said to him, "Lord, are you going to wash my feet?"

⁷ Jesus replied, "You do not realize now what I am doing, but later you will understand."

⁸ "No," said Peter, "you shall never wash my feet."

Jesus answered, "Unless I wash you, you have no part with me."

⁹ "Then, Lord," Simon Peter replied, "not just my feet but my hands and my head as well!"

¹⁰ Jesus answered, "Those who have had a bath need only to wash their feet; their whole body is clean. And you are clean, though not every one of you." ¹¹ For he knew who was going to betray him, and that was why he said not every one was clean.

¹² When he had finished washing their feet, he put on his clothes and returned to his place. "Do you understand what I have done for you?" he asked them. ¹³ "You call me 'Teacher' and 'Lord,' and rightly so, for that is what I am. ¹⁴ Now that I, your Lord and Teacher, have washed your feet, you also should wash one another's feet. ¹⁵ I have set you an example that you should do as I have done for you. ¹⁶ Very truly I tell you, no servant is greater than his master, nor is a messenger greater than the one who sent him. ¹⁷ Now that you know these things, you will be blessed if you do them.

## Study Questions

1. Why did Jesus wash his disciples' feet?

2. How much of serving as a leader involves the ability to trade places either physically or emotionally with the people we lead? Explain.

_____

_____

_____

_____

_____

3. How did Jesus' understanding of himself and who he was help him to serve others? What role should self-awareness and personal perspective play in leaders' willingness to serve and how they serve their team?

_____

_____

_____

_____

_____

# LEADERSHIP INSIGHT AND REFLECTION

What was David's purpose in sharing the spoils with the men who stayed behind? Why did he lead the way he did? What did he hope to gain for himself?

_____

_____

_____

_____

What was Jesus' purpose in leading his disciples? What did he hope to gain himself?

_____

_____

_____

_____

_____

What is your purpose in leading others? What *have* you hoped to gain? What *should* you hope to gain?

_____

_____

_____

_____

_____

_____

_____

_____

# TAKING ACTION

David, the good Samaritan, and Jesus all went out of their way to serve people. How often do you do that? How much is that part of your regular agenda as a leader?

_____

_____

_____

_____

_____

How must you change to become more of a servant leader? What must change in your heart, thinking, and attitude?

_____

_____

_____

_____

_____

_____

What must change in your day-to-day actions?

_____

_____

_____

_____

_____

_____

_____

When and how will you initiate that change?

_____

_____

_____

_____

_____

_____

# GROUP DISCUSSION QUESTIONS

1. How do you think David would have handled the difficult situation he faced had he not "found strength in the LORD his God" (1 Samuel 30:6) or consulted him about going after the raiders? How might things have turned out?

2. Samaritans were despised by the Israelites in Jesus' day. What effect do you think it had on Jesus' listeners when a Samaritan in the parable was willing to serve while a priest and Levite were not?

3. When you come across a person in need or a situation where you could assist others, how do you assess it? When do you step in, and when don't you?

4. How do you know when to step in and serve the people you lead?

5. Why do you think Peter asked Jesus to wash more than his feet? Why do you think Jesus told him no?

6. Are there times when a leader should not serve the people on the team? Explain.

7. How can you become a better servant leader? What action do you believe God is asking you to take in this area? What will you do, and when will you do it?

# LESSON 20

# TEACHABILITY

## To Keep Leading, Keep Learning

## THE QUALITY DEFINED

Whatever made it possible for you to become a leader will qualify you to continue leading. Leaders who are comfortable with the *status quo* will lose influence and effectiveness over time. Therefore, to keep leading, we must keep learning.

Think about it this way:

*Your growth determines who you are.*
*Who you are determines who you attract.*
*Who you attract determines the success of your organization.*

Leaders who want their organization to thrive have to remain teachable. How? By refusing to give in to destination disease. Many people assume that their goals are finish lines. But the reality is that we never arrive at a finish line in life. There is always more of the journey beyond each goal. To keep themselves and their followers moving forward, leaders must continuously grow. To grow, they must learn. To learn, they must remain teachable.

Good leaders understand that past success is no predictor of future success. Every team starts over at the beginning of the season—even after winning the championship. And good leaders know the skills that got them there won't necessarily keep them there. Learning is essential if you want to keep winning.

To be teachable, leaders must not only accept the discomfort of the learning process; they must seek it. Learning anything "from scratch" can be intimidating and hard on a person's pride. But it's impossible to grow without feeling foolish and making mistakes.

So ask yourself when was the last time you tried something for the first time? Your answer will tell you a lot about yourself—and the potential of your future.

# CASE STUDIES

Read these case studies from the Bible and answer the study questions that follow.

## 1 King Nebuchadnezzar Learns the Hard Way

### Daniel 4:4–37

*4 I, Nebuchadnezzar, was at home in my palace, contented and prosperous. 5 I had a dream that made me afraid. As I was lying in bed, the images and visions that passed through my mind terrified me. 6 So I commanded that all the wise men of Babylon be brought before me to interpret the dream for me. 7 When the magicians, enchanters, astrologers and diviners came, I told them the dream, but they could not interpret it for me. 8 Finally, Daniel came into my presence and I told him the dream. (He is called Belteshazzar, after the name of my god, and the spirit of the holy gods is in him.)*

*9 I said, "Belteshazzar, chief of the magicians, I know that the spirit of the holy gods is in you, and no mystery is too difficult for you. Here is my dream; interpret it for me. 10 These are the visions I saw while lying in bed: I looked, and there before me stood a tree in the middle of the land. Its height was enormous. 11 The tree grew large and strong and its top touched the sky; it was visible to the ends of the earth. 12 Its leaves were beautiful, its fruit abundant, and on it was food for all. Under it the wild animals found shelter, and the birds lived in its branches; from it every creature was fed.*

*13 "In the visions I saw while lying in bed, I looked, and there before me was a holy one, a messenger, coming down from heaven. 14 He called in a loud voice: 'Cut down the tree and trim off its branches; strip off its leaves and scatter its fruit. Let the animals flee from under it and the birds from its branches. 15 But let the stump and its roots, bound with iron and bronze, remain in the ground, in the grass of the field.*

*"'Let him be drenched with the dew of heaven, and let him live with the animals among the plants of the earth. 16 Let his mind be changed from that of a man and let him be given the mind of an animal, till seven times pass by for him.*

*17 "'The decision is announced by messengers, the holy ones declare the verdict, so that the living may know that the Most High is sovereign over all kingdoms on earth and gives them to anyone he wishes and sets over them the lowliest of people.'*

*18 "This is the dream that I, King Nebuchadnezzar, had. Now, Belteshazzar, tell me what it means, for none of the wise men in my kingdom can interpret it for me. But you can, because the spirit of the holy gods is in you."*

*19 Then Daniel (also called Belteshazzar) was greatly perplexed for a time, and his thoughts terrified him. So the king said, "Belteshazzar, do not let the dream or its meaning alarm you."*

*Belteshazzar answered, "My lord, if only the dream applied to your enemies and its meaning to your adversaries! 20 The tree you saw, which grew large and strong, with its top touching the sky, visible to the whole earth, 21 with beautiful leaves and abundant fruit, providing food for all, giving shelter to the wild animals, and having nesting places in its branches for the birds— 22 Your Majesty, you are that tree! You have become great and strong; your greatness has grown until it reaches the sky, and your dominion extends to distant parts of the earth.*

*23 "Your Majesty saw a holy one, a messenger, coming down from heaven and saying, 'Cut down the tree and destroy it, but leave the stump, bound with iron and bronze, in the grass of the field, while its roots remain in the ground. Let him be drenched with the dew of heaven; let him live with the wild animals, until seven times pass by for him.'*

*24 "This is the interpretation, Your Majesty, and this is the decree the Most High has issued against my lord the king: 25 You will be driven away from people and will live with the wild animals; you will eat grass like the ox and be drenched with the dew of heaven. Seven times will pass by for you until you acknowledge that the Most High is sovereign over all kingdoms on earth and gives them to anyone he wishes. ²⁶ The command to leave the stump of the tree with its roots means that your kingdom will be restored to you when you acknowledge that Heaven rules. ²⁷ Therefore, Your Majesty, be pleased to accept my advice: Renounce your sins by doing what is right, and your wickedness by being kind to the oppressed. It may be that then your prosperity will continue."*

*²⁸ All this happened to King Nebuchadnezzar. ²⁹ Twelve months later, as the king was walking on the roof of the royal palace of Babylon, ³⁰ he said, "Is not this the great Babylon I have built as the royal residence, by my mighty power and for the glory of my majesty?"*

*³¹ Even as the words were on his lips, a voice came from heaven, "This is what is decreed for you, King Nebuchadnezzar: Your royal authority has been taken from you. ³² You will be driven away from people and will live with the wild animals; you will eat grass like the ox. Seven times will pass by for you until you acknowledge that the Most High is sovereign over all kingdoms on earth and gives them to anyone he wishes."*

*³³ Immediately what had been said about Nebuchadnezzar was fulfilled. He was driven away from people and ate grass like the ox. His body was drenched with the dew of heaven until his hair grew like the feathers of an eagle and his nails like the claws of a bird.*

*³⁴ At the end of that time, I, Nebuchadnezzar, raised my eyes toward heaven, and my sanity was restored. Then I praised the Most High; I honored and glorified him who lives forever.*

> *His dominion is an eternal dominion;*
>> *his kingdom endures from generation to generation.*
> *³⁵ All the peoples of the earth*
>> *are regarded as nothing.*
> *He does as he pleases*
>> *with the powers of heaven*
>> *and the peoples of the earth.*
> *No one can hold back his hand*
>> *or say to him: "What have you done?"*

*36 At the same time that my sanity was restored, my honor and splendor were returned to me for the glory of my kingdom. My advisers and nobles sought me out, and I was restored to my throne and became even greater than before. 37 Now I, Nebuchadnezzar, praise and exalt and glorify the King of heaven, because everything he does is right and all his ways are just. And those who walk in pride he is able to humble.*

## Study Questions

1. What do you believe would have happened if Nebuchadnezzar had been teachable, heeded Daniel's advice, and repented instead of ignoring it for twelve months?

2. How would you describe Nebuchadnezzar's attitude and personality before the prophecy was fulfilled? How would you say he thought of himself?

3. How would you describe him after his sanity was restored?

4. What would you say is the lesson the king learned?

_____

_____

_____

_____

_____

## 2 Naaman Chose Wisely

### 2 Kings 5:1–15

*¹ Now Naaman was commander of the army of the king of Aram. He was a great man in the sight of his master and highly regarded, because through him the LORD had given victory to Aram. He was a valiant soldier, but he had leprosy.*

*² Now bands of raiders from Aram had gone out and had taken captive a young girl from Israel, and she served Naaman's wife. ³ She said to her mistress, "If only my master would see the prophet who is in Samaria! He would cure him of his leprosy."*

*⁴ Naaman went to his master and told him what the girl from Israel had said. ⁵ "By all means, go," the king of Aram replied. "I will send a letter to the king of Israel." So Naaman left, taking with him ten talents of silver, six thousand shekels of gold and ten sets of clothing. ⁶ The letter that he took to the king of Israel read: "With this letter I am sending my servant Naaman to you so that you may cure him of his leprosy."*

*⁷ As soon as the king of Israel read the letter, he tore his robes and said, "Am I God? Can I kill and bring back to life? Why does this fellow send someone to me to be cured of his leprosy? See how he is trying to pick a quarrel with me!"*

*⁸ When Elisha the man of God heard that the king of Israel had torn his robes, he sent him this message: "Why have you torn your robes? Have the man come to me and he will know that there is a prophet in Israel."*
*⁹ So Naaman went with his horses and chariots and stopped at the door of Elisha's house. ¹⁰ Elisha sent a messenger to say to him, "Go, wash yourself*

seven times in the Jordan, and your flesh will be restored and you will be cleansed."

<sup>11</sup> But Naaman went away angry and said, "I thought that he would surely come out to me and stand and call on the name of the LORD his God, wave his hand over the spot and cure me of my leprosy. <sup>12</sup> Are not Abana and Pharpar, the rivers of Damascus, better than all the waters of Israel? Couldn't I wash in them and be cleansed?" So he turned and went off in a rage.

<sup>13</sup> Naaman's servants went to him and said, "My father, if the prophet had told you to do some great thing, would you not have done it? How much more, then, when he tells you, 'Wash and be cleansed'!" <sup>14</sup> So he went down and dipped himself in the Jordan seven times, as the man of God had told him, and his flesh was restored and became clean like that of a young boy.

<sup>15</sup> Then Naaman and all his attendants went back to the man of God. He stood before him and said, "Now I know that there is no God in all the world except in Israel."

## Study Questions

1. Naaman listened to the advice of the young girl who served his wife. What does this tell you about Naaman?

_____

_____

_____

_____

2. When the king of Aram sent Naaman to the king of Israel to be healed, what do you think the Aramean king's motives were?

_____

_____

_____

_____

_____

3. Why did Naaman react angrily when the messenger gave him Elisha's instructions? How did Elisha's treatment of Naaman differ from what the general was used to? What did Naaman expect? Why didn't Elisha greet him?

_____

_____

_____

_____

4. What do you think Naaman learned from this process? Do you think it changed him? If so, how?

_____

_____

_____

_____

_____

_____

## ❸ The Next Lesson

### Mark 10:17–27

*17 As Jesus started on his way, a man ran up to him and fell on his knees before him. "Good teacher," he asked, "what must I do to inherit eternal life?"*

*18 "Why do you call me good?" Jesus answered. "No one is good—except God alone. 19 You know the commandments: 'You shall not murder, you shall not commit adultery, you shall not steal, you shall not give false testimony, you shall not defraud, honor your father and mother.'"*

*20 "Teacher," he declared, "all these I have kept since I was a boy."*

*21 Jesus looked at him and loved him. "One thing you lack," he said. "Go, sell everything you have and give to the poor, and you will have treasure in heaven. Then come, follow me."*

*22 At this the man's face fell. He went away sad, because he had great wealth.*

*23 Jesus looked around and said to his disciples, "How hard it is for the rich to enter the kingdom of God!"*

*24 The disciples were amazed at his words. But Jesus said again, "Children, how hard it is to enter the kingdom of God! 25 It is easier for a camel to go through the eye of a needle than for someone who is rich to enter the kingdom of God."*

*26 The disciples were even more amazed, and said to each other, "Who then can be saved?"*

*27 Jesus looked at them and said, "With man this is impossible, but not with God; all things are possible with God."*

## Study Questions

1. If you had read this passage and stopped at the point where Jesus looked at the man "and loved him" (verse 21), what would you have thought about the man who asked the question? Would you have considered him to be open and teachable?

_____

_____

_____

_____

2. What about after Jesus told him to sell everything, give to the poor, and follow him, and the man walked away sad? How did your view of the man change? Why?

_____

_____

_____

_____

_____

3. What was the real issue for the man, who is identified as a "ruler" in another passage (see Luke 18:18)? Was it wealth? Was it lack of teachability? Was it trust? Was it something else? Explain.

_____

_____

_____

_____

4. How does Jesus' statement that all things are possible with God relate to teachability?

_____

_____

_____

_____

# LEADERSHIP INSIGHT AND REFLECTION

What do Nebuchadnezzar, Namaan, and the man who talked to Jesus all have in common?

_____

_____

_____

_____

_____

_____

How does what they have in common relate to the concept of teachability?

_____

_____

_____

_____

_____

_____

What are the characteristics of a teachable leader?

_____

_____

_____

_____

Which of those characteristics do you possess? Which do you lack? What is keeping you from being a more teachable person and leader?

_____

_____

_____

_____

# TAKING ACTION

If you desire to keep leading and to progress in your leadership role and your career, you need to become teachable. Think about the characteristics of teachability you lack. Which is hindering you the most? Write it here.

_____

_____

_____

What action can you take to change that? What can you do that will remove barriers and open you up to learning and growing? Don't be afraid to ask God to help you in this area.

_____

_____

_____

_____

_____

_____

_____

_____

# GROUP DISCUSSION QUESTIONS

1. How difficult would you have found it to tell the most powerful leader in the world that his "tree" was going to be chopped down and he was going to live like a wild animal? What *do* you do when you are in a position to deliver hard truths or correction to someone in authority?

2. Why do you think Nebuchadnezzar ignored Daniel's advice for so long?

3. Naaman's servants said he would have been willing to do a difficult task if he had been instructed to, but he was hesitant to do something simple. How does this kind of thinking prevent people from growing and learning?

4. Why did Elisha heal Naaman when the man was an Aramean warrior and enemy of Israel? And how does that relate to teachability?

5. The passage you read from Mark 10:17–27 says that Jesus looked at the man who asked him the question and loved him. Why do you think Mark added this detail? How do you think Jesus felt about the man after he walked away sadly?

6. What was your greatest takeaway about teachability from this lesson? How does it relate to leadership?

7. What action do you believe God is asking you to take to become more teachable and grow in your leadership? What will you do? Who will you ask to hold you accountable?

# LESSON 21

# VISION

## You Can Seize Only What You Can See

## THE QUALITY DEFINED

In leadership, vision is utterly indispensable. Why? Because vision *leads leaders*. It paints the target, sparks and fuels the fire within, and draws them forward. And it is also the fire lighter for others who follow that leader. Leaders without vision take their team nowhere worth going. At best, they're traveling in circles. But when leaders have the right vision, they know where to go, and they inspire their people to enthusiastically join them. No vision can be seized until it is first seen by a leader.

But seeing and seizing just any vision is not right. After all, leaders who led evil campaigns probably had vision. Leaders who follow God look for vision that honors him. A vision from God aligns with Scripture, serves people, and makes a positive difference in the world. It should never require the leader or followers to sin. God's vision calls his people to something greater than themselves and always changes the lives of others for the better.

Every vision is unique to the leader in some way, because it draws on their specific gifts, talents, and experiences. No one else can impose it on them. They can't borrow it. In fact, the visionary leader usually senses it as a clear calling from God. It connects to the very depths of who they are and what they believe. And it is their responsibility to discover it, declare it, and lead their people in making it happen.

Above all, a leader's great vision from God is big and far-reaching—much greater than what they could seize alone. The good news is that a God-sized vision acts like a magnet—attracting, challenging, and uniting people. The greater the vision, the more followers and resources it has the potential to attract. And the more challenging it is, the harder the participants are willing to fight to achieve it.

This is how a world-changing vision happens: The leader sees something that could make a huge positive difference but seems impossible; he or she embraces it and calls on those around to join in pursuing it; those others are captivated and inspired to partner with the leader; and together they pursue the vision until they seize it. And the vision rocks the world.

# CASE STUDIES

Read these case studies from the Bible and answer the study questions that follow.

## ① The Vision of Abram

### Genesis 12:1–7

*¹ The LORD had said to Abram, "Go from your country, your people and your father's household to the land I will show you.*

*² "I will make you into a great nation,*
*and I will bless you;*
*I will make your name great,*
*and you will be a blessing.*
*³ I will bless those who bless you,*
*and whoever curses you I will curse;*
*and all peoples on earth*
*will be blessed through you."*

*⁴ So Abram went, as the LORD had told him; and Lot went with him. Abram was seventy-five years old when he set out from Harran. ⁵ He took his wife*

Sarai, his nephew Lot, all the possessions they had accumulated and the people they had acquired in Harran, and they set out for the land of Canaan, and they arrived there.

⁶ Abram traveled through the land as far as the site of the great tree of Moreh at Shechem. At that time the Canaanites were in the land. ⁷ The LORD appeared to Abram and said, "To your offspring I will give this land." So he built an altar there to the LORD, who had appeared to him.

## Genesis 15:1–21

¹ After this, the word of the LORD came to Abram in a vision:

"Do not be afraid, Abram.
    I am your shield,
        your very great reward."

² But Abram said, "Sovereign LORD, what can you give me since I remain childless and the one who will inherit my estate is Eliezer of Damascus?" ³ And Abram said, "You have given me no children; so a servant in my household will be my heir."

⁴ Then the word of the LORD came to him: "This man will not be your heir, but a son who is your own flesh and blood will be your heir." ⁵ He took him outside and said, "Look up at the sky and count the stars—if indeed you can count them." Then he said to him, "So shall your offspring be."

⁶ Abram believed the LORD, and he credited it to him as righteousness.

⁷ He also said to him, "I am the LORD, who brought you out of Ur of the Chaldeans to give you this land to take possession of it."

⁸ But Abram said, "Sovereign LORD, how can I know that I will gain possession of it?"

⁹ So the LORD said to him, "Bring me a heifer, a goat and a ram, each three years old, along with a dove and a young pigeon."

¹⁰ Abram brought all these to him, cut them in two and arranged the halves opposite each other; the birds, however, he did not cut in half. ¹¹ Then birds of prey came down on the carcasses, but Abram drove them away.

*12 As the sun was setting, Abram fell into a deep sleep, and a thick and dreadful darkness came over him. 13 Then the LORD said to him, "Know for certain that for four hundred years your descendants will be strangers in a country not their own and that they will be enslaved and mistreated there. 14 But I will punish the nation they serve as slaves, and afterward they will come out with great possessions. 15 You, however, will go to your ancestors in peace and be buried at a good old age. 16 In the fourth generation your descendants will come back here, for the sin of the Amorites has not yet reached its full measure."*

*17 When the sun had set and darkness had fallen, a smoking firepot with a blazing torch appeared and passed between the pieces. 18 On that day the LORD made a covenant with Abram and said, "To your descendants I give this land, from the Wadi of Egypt to the great river, the Euphrates— 19 the land of the Kenites, Kenizzites, Kadmonites, 20 Hittites, Perizzites, Rephaites, 21 Amorites, Canaanites, Girgashites and Jebusites."*

## Study Questions

1. What was the response of Abram, whom God later renamed "Abraham" (see Genesis 17:5), to the vision he received? What does his response say about him?

_____

_____

_____

_____

2. Why did God appear to Abram again when he arrived in Canaan and repeat his promise? And why did he appear another time after that? What does that say about God?

_____

_____

_____

_____

3. How is Abram's story typical of the challenges leaders face when they have a vision and start to take action to fulfill it? How is Abram's story atypical?

_____

_____

_____

_____

_____

_____

## ❷ The Vision Given to Moses Lasted for Millennia

### Exodus 12:1–29

*¹ The Lord said to Moses and Aaron in Egypt, ² "This month is to be for you the first month, the first month of your year. ³ Tell the whole community of Israel that on the tenth day of this month each man is to take a lamb for his family, one for each household. ⁴ If any household is too small for a whole lamb, they must share one with their nearest neighbor, having taken into account the number of people there are. You are to determine the amount of lamb needed in accordance with what each person will eat. ⁵ The animals you choose must be year-old males without defect, and you may take them from the sheep or the goats. ⁶ Take care of them until the fourteenth day of the month, when all the members of the community of Israel must slaughter them at twilight. ⁷ Then they are to take some of the blood and put it on the sides and tops of the doorframes of the houses where they eat the lambs. ⁸ That same night they are to eat the meat roasted over the fire, along with bitter herbs, and bread made without yeast. ⁹ Do not eat the meat raw or boiled in water, but roast it over a fire—with the head, legs and internal organs. ¹⁰ Do not leave any of it till morning; if some is left till morning, you must burn it. ¹¹ This is how you are to eat it: with your cloak tucked into your belt, your sandals on your feet and your staff in your hand. Eat it in haste; it is the Lord's Passover.*

*¹² "On that same night I will pass through Egypt and strike down every firstborn of both people and animals, and I will bring judgment on all the* gods of Egypt. I am the LORD. *13* The blood will be a sign for you on the houses where you are, and when I see the blood, I will pass over you. No destructive plague will touch you when I strike Egypt.

*14* "This is a day you are to commemorate; for the generations to come you shall celebrate it as a festival to the LORD—a lasting ordinance. *15* For seven days you are to eat bread made without yeast. On the first day remove the yeast from your houses, for whoever eats anything with yeast in it from the first day through the seventh must be cut off from Israel. *16* On the first day hold a sacred assembly, and another one on the seventh day. Do no work at all on these days, except to prepare food for everyone to eat; that is all you may do.

*17* "Celebrate the Festival of Unleavened Bread, because it was on this very day that I brought your divisions out of Egypt. Celebrate this day as a lasting ordinance for the generations to come. *18* In the first month you are to eat bread made without yeast, from the evening of the fourteenth day until the evening of the twenty-first day. *19* For seven days no yeast is to be found in your houses. And anyone, whether foreigner or native-born, who eats anything with yeast in it must be cut off from the community of Israel. *20* Eat nothing made with yeast. Wherever you live, you must eat unleavened bread."

*21* Then Moses summoned all the elders of Israel and said to them, "Go at once and select the animals for your families and slaughter the Passover lamb. *22* Take a bunch of hyssop, dip it into the blood in the basin and put some of the blood on the top and on both sides of the doorframe. None of you shall go out of the door of your house until morning. *23* When the LORD goes through the land to strike down the Egyptians, he will see the blood on the top and sides of the doorframe and will pass over that doorway, and he will not permit the destroyer to enter your houses and strike you down.

*24* "Obey these instructions as a lasting ordinance for you and your descendants. *25* When you enter the land that the LORD will give you as he promised, observe this ceremony. *26* And when your children ask you, 'What does this ceremony mean to you?' *27* then tell them, 'It is the Passover sacrifice to the LORD, who passed over the houses of the Israelites in Egypt and spared our homes when he struck down the Egyptians.'" Then the *people bowed down and worshiped. [28] The Israelites did just what the LORD commanded Moses and Aaron.*

*[29] At midnight the LORD struck down all the firstborn in Egypt, from the firstborn of Pharaoh, who sat on the throne, to the firstborn of the prisoner, who was in the dungeon, and the firstborn of all the livestock as well.*

## Study Questions

1. The message the Lord gave to Moses and Aaron was for immediate action as well as for the future. Why did he do it this way?

 

 

2. The instructions the Lord gave them were highly specific. Why do you think they were so detailed?

 

 

3. How difficult do you think it was for Moses and Aaron to get the children of Israel to listen to these instructions and follow them carefully?

 

 

4. How do you feel when you must communicate to people whom you fear won't accept a far-reaching vision or follow detailed instructions? What do you do to increase the likelihood of success?

_____

_____

_____

_____

_____

## ❸ A Vision for All Time

### Matthew 28:16–20

*16 Then the eleven disciples went to Galilee, to the mountain where Jesus had told them to go. 17 When they saw him, they worshiped him; but some doubted. 18 Then Jesus came to them and said, "All authority in heaven and on earth has been given to me. 19 Therefore go and make disciples of all nations, baptizing them in the name of the Father and of the Son and of the Holy Spirit, 20 and teaching them to obey everything I have commanded you. And surely I am with you always, to the very end of the age."*

### Study Questions

1. Why did Jesus preface his instructions to the disciples with his statement that all authority in heaven and earth had been given to him? How did that information impact their execution of the vision?

_____

_____

_____

_____

_____

_____

2. Why did Jesus also mention that he would be with them? What is the significance of that?

_____

_____

_____

_____

3. How does the directive Jesus gave the eleven disciples impact us today? To whom does it still apply?

_____

_____

_____

_____

4. Why did Jesus wait to communicate this until after he was raised from the dead? Why didn't he do it earlier?

_____

_____

_____

# LEADERSHIP INSIGHT AND REFLECTION

How many different ways did leaders receive vision from God in the passages you read? In how many ways did leaders communicate the vision to the people? Why wasn't it always done in the same way?

_____

_____

_____

_____

_____

_____

How do you think God communicates vision to leaders today?

_____

_____

_____

_____

_____

What vision do you possess for your ministry, family, and career? If you're not sure, spend time in prayer before trying to answer the question.

_____

_____

_____

_____

_____

_____

_____

_____

Look at what you wrote about the vision for your life. How do the different parts of what you wrote work together? Is there a common theme? If so, what is it?

_____

_____

_____

_____

Does what you wrote about the vision for your life require a major transition, or are you already on track for the journey you believe God is asking you to take? If you think you will have to make a major transition, describe it.

_____

_____

_____

_____

_____

# TAKING ACTION

What action can you take immediately to advance the vision God has given you for ministry, family, or career?

_____

_____

_____

_____

_____

_____

_____

_____

What, if anything, is holding you back? How will you overcome it?

_____

_____

_____

_____

_____

_____

_____

_____

When will you take that step? _____

# GROUP DISCUSSION QUESTIONS

1. When you read about people like Abram and Moses who received clear and specific direction from God, how does it make you feel: jealous, frustrated, inspired, afraid? Explain.

2. Abram and his wife Sarai grew impatient when God did not give them a child and tried to force the vision to be fulfilled by producing a child through Sarai's servant (see Genesis 16). How do you handle it when you possess a vision but you have to wait for it to come to fruition?

3. In which part of your life do you possess the clearest picture of what you should be accomplishing? Describe how you came to have that picture.

4. What is your vision for that area? Where are you in the process of achieving it?

5. How much of your vision requires leadership? Describe it.

6. During your current season of life, which would you say is greater: the need for a clear vision, or the need for leadership ability to fulfill it? Explain.

7. What action do you believe God is asking you to take to either receive vision or be able to execute it?

# FINAL GROUP DISCUSSION QUESTIONS

I recommend that you meet together with your group one additional time after you finish the lesson on vision. Before meeting, ask everyone to take some time to reflect on their leadership development since they started the study. Then when you meet, answer the following questions.

1. How would you describe your leadership development journey since you started this process?

2. Have you taken on a greater leadership role or been more proactive as a leader since studying the 21 *Qualities of Leaders in the Bible*? If so, how? If not, why not?

3. How helpful was it to study leadership qualities? How difficult was it to cultivate those qualities to become a better leader?

4. Which of the qualities comes to you most naturally? Why do you think it's easy for you? How can you leverage it to improve your leadership?

5. Which of the qualities do you find most difficult to embody? Why? What can you do to improve it?

6. What is your single greatest takeaway from this learning process?

7. What did you learn from others in the group?

8. How committed are you to further leadership development? How high a priority is it to you on a scale of 1 (low) to 10 (high)?

9. Where do you most want to grow next in your leadership?

# ABOUT THE AUTHOR

John C. Maxwell is a #1 *New York Times* bestselling author, coach, and speaker who has sold more than thirty million books in fifty languages. He has been identified as the #1 leader in business by the American Management Association and the most influential leadership expert in the world by *Business Insider* and *Inc.* magazines. He is the founder of the John Maxwell Company, the John Maxwell Team, EQUIP, and the John Maxwell Leadership Foundation, organizations that have trained millions of leaders from every country of the world. The recipient of the Mother Teresa Prize for Global Peace and Leadership from the Luminary Leadership Network, Dr. Maxwell speaks each year to Fortune 500 companies, presidents of nations, and many of the world's top business leaders. He can be followed at Twitter.com/JohnCMaxwell. For more information about him, visit JohnMaxwell.com.

SUCCESS OR SIGNIFICANCE?
**WHAT'S YOUR STORY?**

MOBILIZING LEADERS FOR
**TRANSFORMATION**

iequip.church | 678.225.3300